Olive Green
English

B1

DARAKWON

The authors of film dialogues and vocabulary lists: Wojciech Wojtasiak, Magdalena Warżała-Wojtasiak

The authors of grammar: Marta Borowiak-Dostatnia (A1-B1), Marcin Mortka (B2-C1)

The authors of interactive dialogues and vocabulary lists: Marta Borowiak-Dostatnia, Monika Glińska

Proofreading: Monika Glińska, Alicja Jankowiak, Natalia Wajda

Edited by: Alicja Jankowiak

Recordings: Graham Crawford, Joanna Haracz-Lewandowska, Jagoda Lembicz, Dale Taylor, Marianna Waters-Sobkowiak

Cover design: Marcin Stanisławski

Graphic design and composition: Wioletta Kowalska / Violet Design

Stock photos: © Fotolia.com

Olive Green English B1

Publisher Chung Kyudo

Editors Cho Sangik, Hong Inpyo, Kim Taeyeon, Kwak Bitna

Designers Kim Nakyung, Yoon Hyunjoo, Im Miyoung

First Published January 2018
By Darakwon Bldg., 211, Munbal-ro, Paju-si, Gyeonggi-do 10881, Republic of Korea
Tel. 82-2-736-2031 (Ext. 550-553)

© Copyright SuperMemo World sp. z o.o., 2018
 SuperMemo is the registered trademark by SuperMemo World sp. z o.o.

© Copyright for the South Korean edition by Darakwon, 2018

All rights reserved. No part of this publication may be reproduced, stored in a retrieval system, or transmitted in any form or by any means, electronic, mechanical, photocopying, or otherwise, without the prior consent of the copyright owner. Refund after purchase is possible only according to the company regulations. Contact the above telephone number for any inquiries.
Consumer damages caused by loss, damage, etc. can be compensated according to the consumer dispute resolution standards announced by the Korea Fair Trade Commission.
An incorrectly collated book will be exchanged.

Price ₩12,000
ISBN: 978-89-277-0953-4 14740
 978-89-277-0950-3 14740 (set)

http://www.darakwon.co.kr
Main Book / Free MP3 Available Online
8 7 6 5 4 3 2 19 20 21 22 23

Table of contents

Introduction **4**

Scene 1 (25): At Russian mafia's **8**
Present Perfect Continuous • Present Perfect Continuous vs. Present Perfect • for vs. since
Interview for an internship • Describing your academic background • Starting a conversation • Steering and structuring a conversation

Scene 2 (26): Gennady and Sergey **18**
First Conditional • unless
Student life • Studying together • Exams • Providing feedback

Scene 3 (27): On a mission with Vlad **28**
should, ought to • to be allowed to, to let, to make somebody do something
Reporting a crime • Describing an incident • Formulating a hypothesis • Presenting arguments • Describing your feelings and general state • Asking for help

Scene 4 (28): At the clothes shop **36**
Second Conditional • the (unique, generic)
Planning your holidays – choosing your destination and route • Walking and cycling tours • Local tourist attractions

Scene 5 (29): Truth about Vlad **44**
used to • would • Comparison: used to, would & Past Simple
Job advertisements • Conditions of employment • Your dream job • Working in the UK – necessary formalities • Cultural differences in the workplace

Scene 6 (30): Hotel hideaway **52**
could • may, might, won't (probability) • will, must (certainty)
Meeting friends after years • Describing memories • Finding out what is new in someone's life • Talking about fulfilled and unfulfilled dreams

Scene 7 (31): Sergey standing guard **60**
Past Perfect • Past Perfect vs. Past Simple
Describing feelings, emotions and general state • Analysing your own behaviour • Offering support

Scene 8 (32): Surprise! **68**
Order of adjectives • -ed, -ing endings for adjectives
Sharing chores and responsibilities with your spouse before Christmas • Holiday shopping • Describing and choosing gifts and holiday decorations

Scene 9 (33): Scuffle at the hotel **76**
Relative pronouns
Telling stories • Expressing interest, surprise, shock and disbelief

Scene 10 (34): Taking hostages **84**
Reported speech
At the airport • Announcements for delayed and cancelled flights

Scene 11 (35): Argument in the park **92**
to be (about) to do • to be on the point/verge/edge of
Development of scientific research and medicine • Using the Internet and social media • Presenting your point of view and the arguments to support it

Scene 12 (36): Vlad's advice **100**
Passive voice • Passive voice with modal verbs
Making a complaint • Returning or exchanging a faulty product • Describing a defect • Describing procedures • Suggesting possible solutions • Expressing dissatisfaction, resentment and gratitude

Translation **108**

Introduction

Olive Green is an innovative course for those who want to learn English from the beginning in a way that is both modern and efficient. It is the perfect combination of fun and effective learning of the highest order.

The **Olive Green** multimedia course is based on an **interactive action film**, where you can decide what course the plot will take, as well as play some arcade-type and language games. The course is divided into 12 film scenes for each language skill level.

What is the best way to learn with the **Olive Green** course?

To begin with, watch the right **film scene** in the multimedia course. We encourage you to watch it several times, so that you can gradually get used to the natural pronunciation you hear and make decisions during interactions. The **subtitles** (available in English and many other languages) will help you understand the content of the dialogue. If you are learning English from scratch, first watch each scene with subtitles in your own language (if available), then with English subtitles, and finally without subtitles. Next, read the **text of the film dialogue** in the book. Then listen to the MP3 recordings of the dialogue, and lastly try to read the text aloud.

Each scene in the book is accompanied by a **list of new words and expressions**. Read them and find them in the dialogue to see how they are used in context, and then listen to the recording of the list.

In the next step, please read the **grammar explanations** describing the most important topics introduced in each film dialogue. You will find many examples of typical applications of all the new structures in these sections.

The multimedia course also includes **interactive dialogues** to let you practice in a variety of communication situations and develop the skills necessary for a conversation in English. Additionally, selected variants of these dialogues have been included in the book, together with the lists of new words and phrases that will help you expand your vocabulary for each topic.

Last but not least, read the **cultural commentary** that will introduce you to some interesting aspects of the culture of the English-speaking countries. The language of the commentaries is simple, but if you are just starting your adventure with English, it may be hard to understand. In that case, please remember that it is always better to try to analyze and understand the general meaning of any English text on your own first – especially if you have been working with the course for some time. Consulting a dictionary for definitions or equivalents of the words that may be new to you should generally be your "second best" option.

To those who wish to continue learning English with **Olive Green**, we recommend the rest part of the course at the other levels.

Enjoy your learning!
The SuperMemo World team
& Darakwon Olive Green team

Olive Green

level B1

Scene 1 (25) Film dialogue and vocabulary

Read the dialogue between Gennady (G), a woman (W), Yuri (Y) and Sergey (S). Check the list of words and phrases below.

> 159,000! (...) Listen, your boy has been gambling heavily for at least half a year, or so ...

G: Mostly dogs ... What do you mean "dogs"? ... Dogs! ... No, I'm not talking about dog races! Dog fights! Your son has not missed a single dog fighting event in over two months!

W: Give me some time! I beg you!

Vocabulary			
gamble	도박하다	dog race	개 경주
heavily	심하게	dog fight	개싸움
half	절반	miss	놓치다
mostly	대부분	month	달, 월
dog	개	beg	애원하다

Olive Green

level B1

What should Gennady do?

G: We're not running a charity here! You will pay your son's debt by tomorrow. If not, my men will pay him a visit. Do we understand each other?

Y: By the way, boss, isn't Sergey coming home today?

G: Tomorrow. He wants me to go to Oxford to witness his graduation. Waste of time if you ask me! But I have got a plan! I have a job for him! An easy one! Perfect for a beginner! And I'm going to team him up with Vlad!

Y: But ... Vlad's a ... Shit, he's a ...

G: A real man! A fighter! A loyal member of this ... organisation. And that is who I want my son to become! So, tomorrow when ... Oh bollocks!

S: Why the hell didn't you come to my graduation? I've been trying to get in touch with you all morning!

G: Sergey, my beloved son!

Vocabulary			
pay a visit	방문하다	fighter	싸움꾼
come home	집에 오다	loyal	충성스러운
witness	증인	member	조직원
graduation	졸업	organization	조직
waste of time	시간 낭비	become	되다
beginner	초급자	Oh hillocks!	헛소리 매!
team up with	팀을 꾸리다	get in touch	연락하다
real	진짜의		

G: All right! You know, I have a son, too, and much like your son he's also a major disappointment! You have got two weeks, yes?

Y: By the way, boss, isn't Sergey coming home today?

G: Tomorrow. He wants me to go to Oxford to witness his graduation. Waste of time if you ask me! But I have got a plan! I have a job for him! An easy one! Perfect for a beginner! And I'm going to team him up with Vlad!

Y: But ... Vlad's a ... Shit, he's a ...

G: A real man! A fighter! A loyal member of this ... organisation. And that is who I want my son to become! So, tomorrow when ... Oh bollocks!

S: Why the hell didn't you come to my graduation? I've been trying to get in touch with you all morning!

G: Sergey, my beloved son!

Vocabulary

major	주요한	real	진짜의
disappointment	실망	fighter	싸움꾼
week	주	loyal	충성스러운
come home	집에 오다	member	조직원
witness	증인	organization	조직
graduation	졸업	become	되다
waste of time	시간 낭비	Oh bollocks!	헛소리 마!
beginner	초급자	get in touch	연락하다
team up with	팀을 꾸리다		

Grammar explanations

현재완료진행

➜ 현재까지 계속되고 있는 행동

I **have been waiting** for you for 20 minutes.
저는 20분 동안 당신을 기다리고 있습니다. (기다리는 사람이 아직 오지 않음)

He **has been painting** the room since this morning.
그는 오늘 아침부터 방에 페인트칠을 하고 있습니다. (아직 끝마치지 못함)

They **have been talking** for over an hour now.
그들은 지금 한 시간 넘게 이야기하는 중입니다. (대화가 아직 끝나지 않음)

➜ 현재에 영향을 미치는 과거의 행동

My hair is wet. I **have been swimming**.
제 머리는 젖어 있습니다. 저는 수영을 하고 있었습니다. (수영이 끝나서 지금은 하고 있지 않음)

David is covered in sweat. He **has been running** with Olive.
David는 땀으로 젖어 있습니다. 그는 Olive와 달리기를 하고 있었습니다. (달리기는 끝났고 몸이 땀으로 젖어 있음)

Sorry I'm late. I **have been driving** in a terrible traffic jam.
늦어서 죄송합니다. 꽉 막힌 도로에서 운전을 하고 있었습니다. (더 이상 운전을 하고 있지 않지만 그러한 운전의 결과로 늦음)

+	I/you/we/they + **have been** + 동사 **-ing** he/she/it + **has been** + 동사 **-ing** Olive **has been working** for him for about two weeks now. Olive는 약 2주 동안 그를 위해 일을 했습니다.
−	I/you/we/they + **haven't been (have not been)** + 동사 **-ing** he/she/it + **hasn't been (has not been)** + 동사 **-ing** They **haven't been seeing** each other for more than a month now. 그들은 한 달 넘게 서로 만나지 않고 있습니다.
?	**Have** + I/you/we/they + **been** + 동사 **-ing** **Has** + he/she/it + **been** + 동사 **-ing** How long **have** you **been staying** at Jessica's? Jessica의 숙소에서 얼마나 머물렀나요? **Have** you **been staying** at Jessica's long? Jessica의 숙소에서 오래 머물렀나요?
+/−	**Yes**, I/you/we/they **have**. **Yes**, he/she/it **has**. **No**, I/you/we/they **haven't (have not)**. **No**, he/she/it **hasn't (has not)**. Have you been waiting for me? Yes, I **have**. 저를 기다리고 있었나요? 네, 그래요. Have you been gambling recently? No, I **haven't**. 최근에 도박을 하셨나요? 아니요, 그렇지 않아요.

Grammar explanations

+

I **have been** doing = I'**ve been** doing

you **have been** doing = you'**ve been** doing

he **has been** doing = he'**s been** doing

we **have been** doing = we'**ve been** doing

you **have been** doing = you'**ve been** doing

they **have been** doing = they'**ve been** doing

−

I **have not been** doing = I'**ve not been** doing = I **haven't been** doing

you **have not been** doing = you'**ve not been** doing = you **haven't been** doing

he **has not been** doing = he'**s not been** doing = he **hasn't been** doing

we **have not been** doing = we'**ve not been** doing = we **haven't been** doing

you **have not been** doing = you'**ve not been** doing = you **haven't been** doing

they **have not been** doing = they'**ve not been** doing = they **haven't been** doing

Remember!
현재완료진행형의 축약형을 사용할 수도 있다.

현재완료진행 vs. 현재완료

현재완료진행

➜ 완료되지 않은 행동

It **has been raining** all day. Don't go out. 하루 종일 비가 내리고 있습니다. 나가지 마세요.

Are you listening to me? I **have been talking** for the last 5 minutes.
제 말을 듣고 있나요? 저는 5분 동안 얘기하고 있어요.

Don't turn the radio off. I **have been listening** to the news.
라디오를 끄지 마세요. 뉴스를 듣고 있는 중이에요.

➜ 행동 기간에 초점을 맞춤

My son **has been wearing** glasses for a week. He can't get used to them.
제 아들은 일주일 동안만 안경을 끼고 있었습니다. 익숙해 할 리가 없어요.

We **have been living** in New York for 5 years now.
현재 우리는 5년 동안 뉴욕에서 살고 있습니다.

They **have been travelling** through the UK since June.
그들은 6월부터 영국 전역을 여행했습니다.

상태동사는 불가!

I ~~have been knowing~~ him for 2 years.
He ~~has been liking~~ the idea of taking part in this project.

현재완료

➜ 완료된 행동

It **has rained** here today. Look, there are some puddles on the street.
오늘 비가 내렸어요. 보세요, 거리에 웅덩이들이 있어요.

I **have talked** to him once or twice recently. 최근에 그와 한두 번 이야기를 나누었습니다.

You can turn the radio off. I **have already listened** to the news.
라디오를 꺼도 좋아요. 이미 뉴스를 들었거든요.

➜ 행동의 결과에 초점을 맞춤

They **have travelled** to all the countries of the British Isles.
저는 영국 제도의 모든 국가를 여행했습니다.

We **have lived** in New York for 5 years now, not in California!
저희는 캘리포니아가 아니라 뉴욕에서 5년 간 살았어요!

My son **has worn** glasses since he was a child. 제 아들은 어렸을 때부터 안경을 썼습니다.

상태동사도 가능!

I **have known** him for 2 years.
저는 2년 동안 그를 알았습니다.

He **has liked** the idea of taking part in this project.
그는 이번 프로젝트에 참여하고자 했습니다.

for와 since

for

➜ 기간

I've been waiting **for** you for 20 minutes. 20분 동안 당신을 기다렸습니다.

He's been living here **for** the last decade.
그는 10년 동안 이곳에서 살고 있습니다.

We have been married **for** 3 years.
저희는 결혼해서 3년 동안 지내고 있습니다.

since

➜ 기준이 되는 시점

I've been waiting for you **since** 3 o'clock. 3시부터 당신을 기다리고 있었습니다.

He's been living here **since** he was born.
그는 태어난 때부터 이곳에서 살고 있습니다.

We have been married **since** 2010.
저희는 2010년에 결혼해서 살고 있습니다.

Communication situations

Read the following dialogues from a job interview.

> We are one of the five top leading hydrology research centres in the world and as such we choose our employees very carefully. You realise, of course, Sergey, that even just a short internship here is a big step forward on your career path. Your educational background is crucial here, so tell us all about it and be precise.

Dialogue 1

Candidate: I see. Shall I start from the nursery school?

HR employee: It won't be necessary. I would like to know more about your secondary school.

Candidate: I was a homeschooler.

HR employee: Why did you opt for homeschooling?

Candidate: Because private tuition was a better solution quality-wise.

HR employee: What made you continue your education?

Candidate: I got a scholarship for my paper on drinking water systems.

HR employee: And the next step in your educational path was university, wasn't it?

Candidate: Yes, it was. I applied to the University of Oxford.

HR employee: How did you manage financially?

Candidate: I was granted a scholarship and spent a year in Africa.

HR employee: And after that?
Candidate: I completed an online Bachelor's Degree programme in Earth Sciences.
HR employee: OK. I see. Have you considered postgraduate or doctorate studies?
Candidate: After completing my MSc in Water Science I'm going to do a PhD.
HR employee: Thank you for your time. We will contact you within a week.

---

internship 인턴쉽 | **big step forward** 커다란 발전 | **career path** 진로 | **crucial** 중대한 | **necessary** 필요한 | **homeschooler** 홈스쿨링하는 사람 | **opt for** ~을 선택하다 | **tuition** 수업료 | **quality-wise** 질적으로 | **financially** 재정적으로 | **scholarship** 장학금 | **paper** 논문 | **Bachelor's Degree** 학사 학위 | **postgraduate** 대학원생 | **doctorate studies** 박사 학위 | **MSc (Master of Science)** 이학 석사 | **PhD (Doctor of Philosophy)** 박사 학위 | **within** 이내에

Dialogue 2

HR employee: Let's start from your secondary school.
Candidate: I attended vocational school.
HR employee: What were you trained in?
Candidate: I decided to learn floral design.
HR employee: Floral design? What made you choose this field of training? Did you see any overlap?
Candidate: I had no plans, just wanted to try something new.
HR employee: And the next step in your educational path was university, wasn't it?
Candidate: No, it wasn't. I decided to have a gap year.
HR employee: And after that?
Candidate: I became a millionaire.
HR employee: Thank you for your time. We will contact you within a week.

---

train 교육시키다 | **floral design** 화훼 장식 | **overlap** 겹치다 | **millionaire** 백만장자

Dialogue 3

Candidate: I graduated from the best secondary school in London.
HR employee: And the next step in your educational path was university, wasn't it?
Candidate: Yes, it was. I was admitted to the department of Earth Sciences at Oxford.
HR employee: How did you manage financially?
Candidate: I had to take a student loan.
HR employee: OK. I see. Have you considered postgraduate or doctorate studies?
Candidate: I want to get some hands-on experience in hydrology first.

department 학과 | **loan** 대출

by heart	암기하여	plumbing	배관
keep up with	~을 따라잡다	with flying colours	뛰어난 성적으로
Master's Degree	석사 학위		

Cultural tips

Did you know that ...?

British universities tend to have a strong reputation internationally due to their history and research. The University of Cambridge and Oxford University are among the most famous UK universities, always ranked in top positions in any rankings. The list of other renowned institutions includes the University College London or King's College London.

Famous U.S. universities include institutions such as Yale, Princeton, Stanford and Harvard, to name just a few.

The photo shows the Harvard Business School.

Scene 2 (26) Film dialogue and vocabulary

Read the dialogue between Gennady (G) and Sergey (S). Check the list of words and phrases below.

You've probably still got my old number.

G: You know how often I need to change these things? If I use the same one for longer than two weeks, the police will come knocking at my door.

S: The police will stop bothering you when you get a normal profession!

G: My profession paid your tuition fees at bloody Oxford and got you the fancy car you came in here! So don't you tell me ... Son, I'm sorry. I screwed up, okay? I'm happy and proud to have a biologist in the family.

S: Hydrologist!

G: Yes, yes, yes – hydrologist! Sit down ... I have a gift for you!

S: What am I supposed to do with it?

G: Shoot!

S: Shoot who?

G: Whoever you wish! ... But keep it within reasonable bounds, okay? I'm so happy this education nightmare is over. In fact, I have a job proposal for you! I want you to help Vlad, our new employee from Russia, find someone ...

S: Dad, please, don't even start!

G: No, listen, it is not what you think! It is a delicate business matter – the police should not get involved. And Vlad is new here. His English is lousy; he does not know the city. Also, he is not bright enough for this kind of job.

level B1

Vocabulary

probably	아마도	whoever	누구든지
knock	두드리다	wish	원하다
normal	평범한	reasonable	적당한
profession	직업	keep within reasonable bounds	적당한 경계를 유지하다
tuition fee	수업료	education	교육
screw up	망치다	job proposal	일자리 제의
be proud (of)	(~을) 자랑스러워 하다	delicate	세심한 주의가 필요한
biologist	생물학자	get involved (in)	(~에) 개입하다
hydrologist	수리학자	lousy	엉망인
gift	선물	city	도시
be supposed to	~하기로 되어 있다		

What should Gennady do?

beg

make a threat

◉ B1-02-02

◉ B1-02-03

G: Son, I beg you! I cannot trust anyone these days! Look, I'm an old man. I'm asking you for help. Mind you, I've been supporting you for years!

S: Okay, dad, just this once! But I'm not doing anything … brutal.

G: Don't worry about that!

G: Son, unless you do it, I will ask you to get a normal profession and start paying back the money I've been giving you for years. That would be what? … A few hundred thousand quid at least. How much does a hydrologist earn these days, huh?

S: Okay, dad, just this once! But I'm not doing anything … brutal.

G: Don't worry about that!

Vocabulary		
	trust	신뢰하다
	Mind you!	그러니까!
	support	부양하다
	once	한번
	brutal	잔혹한
	worry (about)	(~에 대해) 걱정하다

Vocabulary		
	unless	~하지 않는다면
	earn	(돈을) 벌다
	once	한번
	brutal	잔혹한
	worry (about)	(~에 대해) 걱정하다

Grammar explanations

가정법 현재

if + 현재 시제, will
➔ 미래에 일어날 가능성이 있는 행동이나 사건

If I **see** you today, I **will** give you back the book.
오늘 당신을 만나면 책을 돌려 줄게요.

If we **don't hurry**, we **will** miss the bus.
서두르지 않으면 우리는 버스를 놓칠 거예요.

If he **doesn't call** today, I **will not** speak to him anymore.
그가 오늘 전화하지 않으면 저는 더 이상 그와 이야기하지 않겠어요.

If the weather **is** fine at the weekend, they **will** go to the seaside.
주말 날씨가 좋으면 그들은 해변에 갈 거예요.

If you **don't tell** me the truth now, I **will** end our friendship.
지금 제게 진실을 말하지 않으면 우리의 우정을 끝내겠어요.

---

if

➔ 어떤 일이 일어날 수 있다고 생각하는 경우

If you get the information first, will you call me?
당신이 먼저 정보를 얻으면 제게 전화해 줄래요? (하지만 아마도 제가 먼저 정보를 얻게 될 거예요.)

I will prepare some delicious food **if** you come tonight.
당신이 오늘 밤에 온다면 제가 맛있는 음식을 준비해 놓을게요. (오늘 올 건가요? 잘 모르겠군요.)

If Robert finds Olive, he will hurt her.
Robert는 Olive를 찾으면 그녀를 해칠 거예요.
(Robert가 Olive를 찾지 못할 가능성이 커요.)

➔ if: '때때로'의 의미

If you exercise regularly, you will see a difference.
규칙적으로 운동을 하면 차이가 느껴질 거예요.

When you exercise regularly, you will see a difference.
규칙적으로 운동을 할 때마다 차이가 느껴질 거예요.

when

➔ 어떤 일이 일어날 것임을 알고 있는 경우

When you get the information, will you call me?
당신이 먼저 정보를 얻으면 제게 전화해 줄래요? (당신이 정보를 얻게 될 것이라는 점을 알고 있어요.)

I will prepare some delicious food **when** you come.
당신이 온다면 제가 맛있는 음식을 준비해 놓을게요.
(저는 당신이 오늘 올 것이라는 점을 알고 있어요.)

When Robert finds Olive, he will hurt her.
Robert는 Olive를 찾으면 그녀를 해칠 거예요.
(Robert는 Olive를 찾을 거예요. 그것은 시간 문제죠.)

➔ when: '언제나'의 의미

If I'm hungry, I'll go to my mum. She's the best cook!
배가 고프면 저는 엄마에게 갈 거예요. 엄마는 최고의 요리사니까요!

When I'm hungry, I'll go to my mum. She's the best cook!
배가 고플 때마다 저는 엄마에게 갈 거예요. 엄마는 최고의 요리사니까요!

unless

unless = if ... not

I will not use this gun **unless** I need to do so.
그럴 필요가 없다면 저는 이 총을 사용하지 않을 거예요.
= I will not use this gun **if** I do **not** need to do so.

Unless she gives the documents back, she will have to live in fear.
그녀가 문서를 되돌려 주지 않으면 그녀는 두려움 속에서 살아야 할 거예요.
= **If** she does **not** give the documents back, she will have to live in fear.

It will be difficult to deal with Olive **unless** I ask Gennady for help.
Gennady에게 도움을 요청하지 않으면 Olive와의 거래는 힘들 거예요.
= It will be difficult to deal with Olive **if** I do **not** ask Gennady for help.

Robert will not know about Olive's further steps **unless** David tells him.
David가 말을 해 주지 않으면 Robert는 Olive의 다음 계획에 대해 알지 못할 거예요.
= Robert will not know about Olive's further steps **if** David does **not** tell him.

Communication situations

Read the following dialogues between students preparing for an exam.

> I'm afraid of this exam. They say it's one of the most difficult ones. I've been learning long and hard but I'm still not sure if I'm ready.

Dialogue 1

Student B: I know what you mean. Let's revise it again together.

Student A: That's a very good idea. So ... Hmm, I know. How about a quiz formula: a short description of a system or an organ followed by an answer.

Student B: OK. Let me start.

Student A: All right. Can we begin with the skeleton? That's my favourite part.

Student B: Be my guest. What's the name of the only bone in your skull that moves?

Student A: Easy! It's the jawbone! My turn. How many bones have you got in your hands?

Student B: In my two hands?

Student A: Yes, unless you've got three or more. Come on!

Student B: 54 altogether.

Communication situations

Student A: Can you group them?

Student B: Yes. There are 2 in the thumb plus 3 in each finger plus 5 in the palm and also 8 wrist bones.

Student A: Wow, impressive! You're very well prepared!

---

revise 복습하다 I formula 공식 I Be my guest. 원하는 대로 하세요. I skeleton 해골 I skull 두개골 I jawbone 턱뼈 I thumb 엄지손가락 I palm 손바닥 I wrist 손목

Dialogue 2

Student B: I understand you perfectly. Why don't we go through it together?

Student A: That's a very good idea. So ... Hmm, I know. How about a quiz formula: a short description of a system or an organ followed by an answer.

Student B: Sure, why not. Shall we?

Student A: Yeah, I'm ready. Let's cover the circulatory system first.

Student B: What do you call the two main blood vessel systems?

Student A: Systemic veins and systemic arteries.

Student B: What's the function of the veins?

Student A: They take the blood back to the heart.

Student B: Well done! I always confuse those two systems!

Student A: Oh no, really? You have to be really careful during the exam then!

---

go through 검토하다 I circulatory 순환의 I vessel 혈관 I systemic 전신의 I heart 심장; 마음 I confuse 헷갈리다, 혼란시키다

Dialogue 3

Student B: What is the main function of the organs in the respiratory system?

Student A: Well, depends on which organs you have in mind.

Student B: Let's start with the nasal cavity.

Student A: You want to talk about the nose? OK. It prepares the air before it goes into the lungs.

Student B: Yes, it cleans, warms and moisturizes the air.

Student A: Yes, that's it. Now onto the next question …

---

respiratory system 호흡계 | **nasal cavity** 비강 | **lungs** 폐 | **moisturize** 수분을 제공하다

Vocabulary plus

chamber	(생명체 내의) 실	pee	오줌을 누다
cranium	두개골	pipe	관, 파이프
disgusting	역겨운	rib	갈비(뼈)
excess water	지나친 물기	scope	범위
expel	퇴학시키다	shape	모양
for one's own good	~을 위해	supply	공급하다
go ahead	시작하다	trachea	기도
indeed	정말, 아주	urine	소변
kidney	신장	valve	판막
lobe	(인체 기관) 엽	vertebra	척추
oxygen	산소	windpipe	(호흡) 기관

Cultural tips

Did you know that ...?

London is by far the largest city in England and the United Kingdom, and it is the capital of the United Kingdom. It is located on the River Thames. London is one of the world's most important cities for business, finance and politics. It's also important for culture: media, entertainment, fashion and art. The city has a huge network of transport systems, and the London Underground was the world's first underground railway system.

The photo shows the Houses of Parliament and Big Ben in London.

Scene 3 (77) — Film dialogue and vocabulary

Read the dialogue between Sergey (S) and Vlad (V). Check the list of words and phrases below.

Vlad, could you remove your elbow from the lever?

S: I'll go and have a look. You stay in the car, okay? And let me make this clear: you are not allowed to touch any buttons! Basically, just sit and don't do anything! No, Vlad! You ought to stay in the car! We don't want to draw anyone's attention! Blending in – this is what we're aiming for! Okay? What? What do you want?

V: Your gun! Take it! A small man should have a gun!

Vocabulary			
remove	치우다	touch	만지다
elbow	팔꿈치	button	버튼
lever	(자동차) 변속 레버	draw attention	관심을 끌다
make clear	분명하게 하다	blend in	(주위 환경에) 섞여들다
be allowed to	~하도록 허락 받다	aim for	~을 목표로 하다

Read the dialogue between the guard (G), Vlad and Sergey (S). Check the list of words and phrases below.

Sir, please remove your vehicle! You're not allowed to park there!

Not my car!

G: But I saw you sitting in it and talking to the driver. Please call him and make him move it! Now! (...) Sir, please stop right now! (...) You leave me no choice!

S: I'm awfully sorry, sir. What seems to be the problem?

| vehicle | 차량 | move | 움직이다 |
| driver | 운전자 | | |

Grammar explanations

should와 ought to

→ 해야 할 일이나 옳다고 생각하는 바를 말할 때
→ 조언을 구할 때

should

It's late. We **should go** home now.
늦었어요. 이제 집으로 가야 해요.

He looks tired. He **should take** a day off. 그는 피곤해 보여요. 하루 쉬어야 해요.

Sport is the best. I **should do** more exercises. 운동이 최고예요. 저는 운동을 더 해야 해요.

What **should** I **do** now? I need some help.
이제 제가 무엇을 해야 하나요? 제게는 도움이 필요해요.

ought to

On hot days like today you **ought to drink** more water.
오늘과 같이 더운 날에는 물을 더 많이 마셔야 해요.

He **ought to apologize** for the words he has said.
그는 자신이 한 말에 대해 사과해야 해요.

You **ought to rest** now. You have been working too much recently.
당신은 이제 쉬어야 해요. 요즘 일을 너무 많이 했어요.

+ I/you/he/she/it/we/they + **should/ought to** + 동사 원형

She **should be** more careful about what she says when David is around.
David가 주변에 있을 때 그녀는 자신이 하는 말에 대해 보다 주의를 기울여야 해요.

He **ought to report** everything to Robert. 그는 Robert에게 모든 것을 보고해야 해요.

− I/you/he/she/it/we/they + **should not (shouldn't)** + 동사 원형
I/you/he/she/it/we/they + **ought not to (oughtn't to)** + 동사 원형

Olive **should not (shouldn't) trust** David too much.
Olive는 David를 너무 믿어서는 안 돼요.

Actually, she **ought not to trust** him at all! 사실, 그녀는 그를 절대로 믿지 말아야 해요!

? Should + I/you/he/she/it/we/they + 동사 원형

Should Sergey **take** the gun from Vlad? Sergey가 Vlad에게서 총을 뺏어야 하나요?

Ought + I/you/he/she/it/we/they + to + 동사 원형

Ought Vlad **to stay** in the car, as Sergey wants?
Sergey가 원하는 대로 Vlad는 차에 있어야 하나요?

+/− Yes, I/you/he/she/it/we/they **should / ought to**.
No, I/you/he/she/it/we/they **should not (shouldn't) / ought not to (oughtn't to)**.

Should I **go** now? Yes, you **should**. 제가 지금 가야 하나요? 네, 그래야 해요.

Ought we **to turn** left then? No, you **oughtn't to**. Turn right.
이제 좌회전을 해야 하나요? 아니요, 그러면 안 돼요. 우회전하세요.

Remember!

should = ought to
→ **should**와 **ought to**는 의미가 같지만 **should**가 더 많이 사용되는 편이고 **ought to**는 보다 정중한 의미를 나타내고자 할 때 사용된다.

be allowed, let, make

be allowed to = ~하는 것이 허용되다, ~하는 것을 허락받다

You **are not allowed to** **take** photos here. 이곳에서는 사진을 찍으실 수 없습니다.

I **was allowed to** **enter** the building. 저는 건물로 들어가도록 허락받았습니다.

We **are not allowed to** **smoke** in the flat but we **are allowed to** **have** parties.
아파트에서의 흡연은 허가되지 않지만 파티를 여는 것은 허가됩니다.

let = ~하게 하다, 시키다

Our boss **lets** **us use** the Internet at work but within reasonable boundaries.
사장님께서는 근무 시간 내 인터넷 사용을 허용하시지만 그럴만한 이유가 있는 경우에만 가능합니다.

Let **me see** it. 제가 한번 볼게요.

Why don't you **let** **us do** the work for you? 저희가 당신을 위해 그 일을 할까요?

make = ~하도록 만들다, 억지로 시키다

Robert **made** **David take** the phone. Robert는 David가 전화를 받도록 시켰습니다.

His beautiful song **made** **me cry**. 그의 아름다운 노래가 저를 울렸습니다.

Good teachers **don't make** **their students learn** by heart.
훌륭한 교사는 학생들에게 암기를 강요하지 않습니다.

They **make** **the students understand** the lesson. 그들은 학생들이 수업 내용을 이해하도록 만듭니다.

Communication situations

Read the following dialogues between a policeman and a victim reporting a crime.

Have a seat, please. I need to take a statement from you and it may take some time. So let's start. Could you describe what happened?

Dialogue 1

Victim: I am still shaking because I have been mugged.

Police officer: I understand. It's not a nice feeling. When and where were you mugged?

Victim: It all happened two hours ago in a street near my house.

Police officer: All right. And where do you live?

Victim: I live in Queen Street.

Police officer: Did you see the criminal?

Victim: No, everything happened too fast.

Police officer: In that case our investigation is closed. There is no chance of finding the mugger.

---

be mugged 강도 당하다 | **find** 찾아내다

Dialogue 2

Victim: We had a burglary when we were on holidays.

Police officer: What makes you think so?

Victim: Well, I'm sure somebody broke into the house because it was one big mess when we arrived.

Police officer: What about your neighbours? Did anybody see anything?

Victim: No, I don't think so. Otherwise somebody would have reported the burglary.

Police officer: Maybe yes, maybe no. We'll interview your neighbours shortly. Let's talk about the theft now. Is anything missing?

Victim: Yes, two paintings from my private collection.

Police officer: You've got a private collection and yet you have no burglar alarm installed?

Victim: The burglar alarm outside the house was cut off.

Police officer: All right. It proves that the burglars were professionals.

burglary 도둑 | **mess** 엉망인 상태 | **neighbour** 이웃 | **shortly** 곧 | **theft** 절도 | **missing** 없어진 | **cut off** 절단하다

Dialogue 3

Victim: I was one of the hostages in that bank robbery last week.

Police officer: OK, I see. Please, have a glass of water. You seem very upset. Is there something or someone bothering you? Do you need psychological counselling?

Victim: Yes, maybe I need some help. I either can't sleep or have nightmares.

Police officer: I understand. Give me a second and I'll get in touch with our psychologist.

hostage 인질 | **bank robbery** 은행 강도 | **psychological counselling** 정신 상담 | **psychologist** 정신과 의사

Vocabulary plus

accuse of	~의 죄로 고소하다
acquitted of all charges	모든 혐의가 무죄로 선고된
bystander	행인
CCTV	폐쇄 회로 TV
citizen	시민
commit a crime	범죄를 저지르다
common problem	흔한 문제
convict	~에게 유죄를 선고하다
convinced	확신하는
couple	둘
debit card	직불 카드
dislike	싫어하다
express	표현하다
fine	벌금을 부과하다
fraud	사기
guilty	유죄의
highly unlikely	매우 가능성이 낮은
How dare you!	어떻게 감히!
ID (identity card)	신분증
identify	확인하다, 알아보다
I'm blank.	깜빡 잊었습니다.
in broad daylight	대낮에
in custody	구류되어
in the long run	결국
incident	사건
industrial espionage	산업 스파이
inside job	내부 범죄
insure	보험에 들다
jargon	용어
jealousy	질투
jump to conclusions	속단하다
juvenile delinquent	미성년 범죄자, 비행 청소년
law and order	법과 질서
life imprisonment	종신형
likely	가능성 있는
live off	~에 의지해서 살다
lock up	~을 철장 안에 가두다
loss	분실
lover	애인
motivate	~에 동기를 주다
motive	동기
mugging	강도
My apologies.	죄송합니다.
No wonder.	당연하다.
offender	범죄자
papers	서류
pensioner	연금 수급자
perfectly fine	정말 괜찮은
petty crime	경범죄
plead not guilty	범행을 부인하다
prime suspect	유력한 용의자
promote	승진시키다
purse	지갑
quite the opposite	정반대
release	풀어 주다
release on bail	보석금으로 석방시키다
relevant	관련 있는
seek revenge (on)	~에 대해 보복하다
sentence	판결
serve	복역하다
single offence	단행범
study	서재
substantial	상당한
take a deep breath	심호흡하다
take to court	~을 법정에 세우다
That's none of your business.	상관하지 마세요.
too soon to tell	말하기 너무 이른
walk free	처벌을 받지 않고 (자유롭게) 걸어서 나가다
Who do you take me for?	날 뭘로 보는 거야?

Cultural tips

Did you know that ...?

On-road parking (waiting) restrictions are indicated by yellow lines at the edge of roads, usually accompanied by a sign indicating when parking is prohibited, e.g. "Mon-Sat 8 am–6:30 pm" or "At any time". If no days are indicated on the sign, restrictions are in force every day, including public holidays and Sundays.

Scene 4 (28) Film dialogue and vocabulary

Read Vlad's monologue. Check the list of words below.

I go in and ... talk to them! We talk, we find a ... solution! I come back! You watch the door. They come out, you stop them!

B1-04-01

| solution | 해결책 |

Read the dialogue between Olive (O) and David (D). Check the list of words and phrases below.

One thing that always puzzles me is the popularity of polo shirts among men. Why would anyone want to wear one?

B1-04-02

36 Olive Green

level **B1**

O: They make you look ... well, unmanly would be the word. And the popped collar, dear god! It's a fashion crime! Look! You'd look so much better if you wore a plain T-shirt ... Black, white. Maybe even red ... Though red ... I'd have to see you in it first.

D: Olive, would it be okay if you just left me alone for a second?

Vocabulary

puzzle	혼란시키다	fashion crime	패션 범죄 (패션에서 해서는 안 되는 것)
popularity	인기	T-shirt	티셔츠
polo shirt	폴로 셔츠 (깃이 있는 반팔 셔츠)	black	검정색
unmanly	남자답지 못한	white	흰색
popped collar	세운 깃	red	빨간색
Dear God!	신이시여!		

Read Vlad's monologue. Check the list of words below.

The polo shirt! A horrible invention! What do you think? Would I look like a Brit in a shirt like this? Would I ... blend in ... Olive?

horrible	끔찍한	shirt	셔츠
invention	발명품		

Olive and David run out of the shop. Read David's monologue.

Read Vlad's monologue.

Grammar explanations

가정법 과거

if + 과거 시제, would
→ 상상이나 가정에 의한, 혹은 비현실적인 현재 및 미래의 상황

If I **went** on a trip around the world, I **would** be the happiest person in the world.
제가 세계 여행을 하고 있다면 저는 세상에서 가장 행복한 사람일 거예요. (현재 여행하고 있지 않음)

If we **didn't work** so hard, we **would** have time for our hobbies. 우리가 그처럼 열심히 일하지 않는다면 취미 활동을 할 수 있는 여가 시간이 있을 거예요. (열심히 일을 하고 있어서 취미 활동을 할 수 있는 시간이 없음)

If they **won** a lottery ticket, they **would** make all their dreams come true.
그들이 복권에 당첨된다면 자신들의 꿈을 실현시킬 수 있을 거예요. (복권 당첨을 원하지만 그런 일은 일어나지 않음)

→ 문장 구조

if + 과거 시제, would: **If** I had a lot of money, I would travel more. 제게 돈이 많다면 저는 여행을 더 많이 다니겠어요.

would + if + 과거 시제: I would travel more **if** I had a lot of money. (콤마 없음)

→ if절에서는 I/he/she/it의 동사로 were를 사용할 수 있다.

If I/he/she **were** a rich man ... 내가/그가/그녀가 만약 부자라면…

정관사 the

→ 유일무이한 대상: 대상이 오직 하나뿐인 경우

the environment 자연 환경
the Queen (in a country) (한 나라의) 여왕
the government 정부
the Prime Minister 수상
the Sun, the Earth, the Moon 태양, 지구, 달
cf. Mars, Venus, Neptune 등은 무관사

→ 일반적인 대상 (the + 단수 명사): 하나의 대상이 전체를 대표하는 경우 (동물, 발명, 발견 등)

The cheetah is the fastest of land animals. 치타는 육상 동물 중에서 가장 빠른 동물입니다.
The dog barks when it is ready to fight. 개는 싸울 준비가 되면 짖습니다.
The fish needs oxygen in the water to breathe. 물속에서 호흡하기 위해 물고기는 산소를 필요로 합니다.
The electron is still studied by scientists. 전자는 과학자들에 의해 계속 연구되고 있습니다.
The smartphone has changed the world in recent years. 최근 몇 년 동안 스마트폰이 세상을 바꿔놓고 있습니다.
The aspirin helps with headaches. 아스피린은 두통에 도움을 줍니다.

Communication situations

Read the following dialogues between a couple planning this year's holidays.

I'm tired of hotels, all-inclusive packages and swimming pools. Let's do something different this year. Why don't we show the kids a bit of wild countryside?

Dialogue 1

Husband: Yes, I feel the same. We need a change.

Wife: So, any ideas? Maybe a walking tour?

Husband: Sure. Let's go on the Internet and find some tailor-made tours.

Wife: That's not the point. There is no difference between the "all-inclusive" and "tailor-made" holidays. Both are very posh and predictable.

Husband: Actually, what would you say to a cycling tour?

Wife: Sure. Have you got one in mind?

Husband: Actually, yes. The Coast to Coast Cycle Route.

Wife: Sounds interesting. Let's go on the Internet and check the details.

Husband: They suggest starting from the west coast of Cumbria here.

Wife: Excellent. I have never been to Cumbria.

Husband: Good. We could then cross the Lake District and end up on the northeast coast, at Sunderland.

Wife: I love that plan. Let's take our time and go slowly, to really take it all in. It's going to be fantastic.

tailor-made 맞춤의 | predictable 예측 가능한 | cycling tour 자전거 여행 | route 길 | west 서쪽 | take one's time 천천히 하다

Dialogue 2

Husband: I'm glad you said so. It's a good idea.

Wife: Why don't we have a look at some footpaths here, in the UK? I've heard about the Robin Hood Way. What do you think?

Husband: I think the kids may like it.

Wife: Wait, I'll just try to find the right website. OK, let's have a look here.

Husband: It runs for 168 km. Isn't it too long for us?

Wife: Right. That is quite a long distance for a bunch of beginners.

Husband: Well, we can walk just a part of the whole distance.

Wife: Then I'd do the most exciting part. Do you think we could camp in Sherwood?

Husband: No ... But we could go there when the Robin Hood Festival takes place.

Wife: That's a brilliant idea! Let me see ... It's in August. Perfect time for a holiday!

footpath 오솔길 | website 웹사이트 | bunch 무리, 떼 | exciting 신나는 | camp 야영하다

Dialogue 3

Husband: How about the 1066 Country Walk?

Wife: I have never heard about it. Tell me more.

Husband: It starts in an old picturesque village and runs through the south east of England.

Wife: "Pevensey", right? Like those children from Narnia?

Husband: Yes. And the countryside hasn't changed much since the 15th century. Sounds amazing.

Wife: Still, it seems a pity to visit the South and yet ignore the coast and the ocean.

Husband: You can't have your cake and eat it.

picturesque 그림 같은 | east 동쪽 | countryside 시골 지역 | coast 해안 | have your cake and eat it 두 마리 토끼를 다 잡다

Vocabulary plus

at once	즉시	keep	~에 있다
be eager to	~하고 싶어 하다	look up	방문하다
beach	해변	oak	오크 (나무)
beforehand	사전에	promising	유망한
break down (into)	(~으로) 구분하다	set off	출발하다
castle	성	shame	아쉬운 일
classified	분류된	southern	남쪽의
coach	대형 버스	Special Area of Conservation	특별 보전 지역
commemorate	기념하다	stand	참다, 견디다
consider	고려하다	stay overnight	하룻밤 묵다
deer	사슴	take in	이해하다
either way	어느 쪽이든	themed	특정 테마의 분위기를 살린
informative	유익한	trail	오솔길
inn	여관		

Cultural tips

Did you know that …?

Sherwood Forest is a forest in England, famous for its association with the legend of Robin Hood. Every August the place becomes a spot for the Robin Hood Festival that lasts a week. This event recreates the atmosphere of the Middles Ages and gathers major characters from the legend.

Scene 5 (29) — Film dialogue and vocabulary

Read the dialogue between Sergey (S) and Gennady (G). Check the list of words and phrases below.

A loose cannon, dad! That's what he is! A mindless lunatic! Where the hell did you find him?

G: Listen! I've known Vlad for 25 years! And you know what? He saved my life once! We met in Russia in 1988. It was during Perestroika … Clever people could get rich quickly. I was like that. Vlad was a boy then, 18 years old, already a huge man, but he was very poor. He used to … eat the leftovers from bins behind the posh hotels … Sergey, you have no idea what poverty can do to your mind! … Anyway, I took him under my wing … He would collect debts for me, run errands … Also, he used to work as my bodyguard. One day, I was concluding a transaction with a few gentlemen. I thought they were friends, but it was a trap!

level B1

One minute we were talking and drinking, and suddenly they all had knives in their hands. Before I noticed, I had one in my stomach. And you know what Vlad did? Five men! With his bare hands! Then he carried me to hospital. They told me later that he was walking through the streets of Moscow all covered in blood ... like a demon! The point is I owe him a lot, yes? And you know ... there have been some ... personal tragedies in his life lately. He came to the UK because he had no choice. He hates being here. He's ... well ... depressed, I guess. So, I want you to teach him some English, show him things ... help him finish this job! He needs to work! You leave him with nothing to do, he sits in a hotel room, looking at the wall. It is sad! I want him to be happy again!

S: Okay, I can be his driver! But promise me this – I am not helping him kill anyone!

G: No! He'll give them a scare, take back what they have stolen. ... Okay, he may beat them up a little bit! But I promise you he's not killing anyone!

S: Come Vlad! Let's go and get them!

Vocabulary

loose cannon	예측불허의 인물	gentleman	신사
mindless	아무 생각 없는	trap	함정
lunatic	미치광이	knife	칼
save	구하다	carry	데리고 가다
during	~ 동안에	hospital	병원
quickly	빠르게	walk	걷다
huge	거대한	street	길
leftovers	남은 음식	blood	피
posh	화려한	demon	악마
hotel	호텔	point	요점
poverty	가난	personal	개인적인
take under one's wing	보호하다	tragedy	비극
collect	모으다	lately	최근에
run errands	심부름을 하다	hate	싫어하다
used to	~하곤 했다	depressed	낙담한
bodyguard	경호원	wall	벽
conclude	끝마치다	give a scare	겁주다
transaction	거래		

Grammar explanations

used to

→ 과거에 규칙적으로 발생했던 일이지만 현재는 그렇지 않은 경우 (과거의 습관이나 상태)

Vlad **used to** work only in Moscow. Vlad는 한때 모스크바에서만 일을 했습니다.

He **used to** be poor. 그는 한때 가난했습니다.

He **used to** deal with most of Gennady's business. 그는 한때 Gennady의 사업 대부분을 담당했습니다.

Olive **used to** have a normal job but she got bored with it after a short while.
Olive는 한때 평범한 직업을 가졌지만 얼마 후 그 일에 싫증을 느끼게 되었습니다.

Olive **used to** work for Cloutier. Olive는 한때 Cloutier를 위해 일했습니다.

−	**didn't + use to** **did not + use to** She **didn't use to** take a train to work. She worked in the same town where she lived. 그녀는 기차를 타고 출근하지 않았습니다. 그녀는 그녀가 살던 도시에서 일을 했습니다. A hundred years ago people **didn't use to** use computers (because there weren't any). 백 년 전 사람들은 (없었기 때문에) 컴퓨터를 사용하지 않았습니다. As a young couple we **didn't use to** go skiing every winter. We didn't have money for that. 젊은 부부였던 저희는 매년 스키를 타러 가지 않았습니다. 그럴 만한 돈이 없었습니다.
?	**Did … use to …?** **Did** he **use to** live in the USA? 그가 미국에서 살았던 적이 있나요? **Did** you **use to** smoke? 담배를 피우신 적이 있나요? **Did** they **use to** visit this holiday resort every year? 그들이 매년 이 휴가지를 방문했었나요?
+/−	Did you use to smoke? 담배를 피우신 적이 있나요? **Yes**, I **did**. Luckily I quit 5 years ago. 네, 있어요. 다행히도 5년 전에 끊었어요. Did he use to repair the car by himself? 그가 혼자서 차를 수리한 적이 있나요? **No**, he **didn't (did not)**. He never liked tinkering. 아니요, 없어요. 그는 어설프게 손보는 것을 결코 좋아하지 않았어요.

would와 used to

➔ **used to**와 마찬가지로 **would** 역시 과거에 규칙적으로 발생했던 일을 나타내지만, **would**는 아래의 경우에 사용된다.
- 현재에도 일어날 가능성이 있는 경우
- 과거의 습관 (과거의 상태 ➔ **used to**)
- 의문문과 부정문에서는 사용되지 않음

We **would** swim in that lake when we were kids. 우리는 어렸을 때 저 호수에서 수영을 하곤 했습니다.
= We **used to** swim in that lake when we were kids.

I **would** do silly things as a teenager. 저는 십대일 때 어리석은 짓을 하곤 했습니다.
= I **used to** do silly things as a teenager.

We **used to** believe that we could change the world. 저희는 저희가 세상을 바꿀 수 있으리라 생각했습니다.

They **used to** love this campsite. 그들은 이 캠프장을 좋아했습니다.

I **used to** know all the key historical dates from the Middle Ages. 저는 한때 중세 시대의 주요한 역사적인 날짜를 모두 알고 있었습니다.

She **used to** be a chain smoker at university. 그녀는 대학에 다닐 때 골초였습니다.

used to/would와 과거 시제

used to	would	과거 시제
➔ 반복적인 과거의 습관 및 행동, 혹은 상태	➔ 반복적인 과거의 행동	➔ 일시적인 과거의 행동
I **used to** work as a chef in that restaurant. 저는 한때 저 식당에서 주방장으로 일을 했습니다.	I **would** play football almost every afternoon as a child. 저는 어렸을 때 거의 매일 오후 축구를 했습니다.	I **met** him a few years ago. 저는 몇 년 전에 그를 만났습니다.
We **used to** have lunch together on every Sunday. 저희는 일요일마다 함께 점심을 먹곤 했습니다.	Even as an adult he **would** call his parents whenever he was on holiday. 그는 비록 성인이었지만 휴일 마다 부모님께 전화를 드렸습니다.	My mom **baked** a delicious cake yesterday. 엄마가 어제 맛있는 케이크를 만들어 주었습니다.
She **used to** enjoy going to parties. 그녀는 한때 파티에 가는 것을 좋아했습니다.	Our dog **would** always bark at guests. 저희 개는 항상 손님을 보면 짖었습니다.	She **knocked** on the door twice. 그녀는 두 차례 노크를 했습니다.

Communication situations

Read the following dialogues. Vlad and Gennady are discussing Vlad's first job in the UK.

Vlad, I'm glad you have come to England. Finally. I need you here. But before you start working for me, there are some legal issues we have to deal with. We have to make you visible and recognizable for the British system. Then we'll figure out a job for you.

Dialogue 1

Vlad: A job for me? Am I not supposed to work for you?

Gennady: Eventually - yes. But first you must appear in all the right British databases as a legally working foreigner. What would you like to do?

Vlad: I can do anything as long as it's good money.

Gennady: Hmm, yes. Remember that they've got a salary and a wage here.

Vlad: Are people paid overtime here?

Gennady: Generally – yes.

Vlad: "Generally"? So are you paid or not?

Gennady: When you work for me, you don't do overtime. It's a performance-oriented job, so no overtime is paid. But in regular companies overtime wages are usually paid, yes.

---

visible (눈에) 보이는 | **recognizable** 인식할 수 있는 | **eventually** 결국 | **database** 데이터베이스 | **foreigner** 외국인 | **salary** 봉급 | **wage** 임금 | **overtime** 초과 근무 | **performance-oriented** 성과 위주의

Dialogue 2

Vlad: All right, boss. What's the first step?

Gennady: Have you got a NINO?

Vlad: I don't think so. What is it?

Gennady: National Insurance Number - an obligatory document that makes you recognizable for the British system. I'll see about that. Now, what about a work permit?

Vlad: Well, if I don't have this NINO thing, I don't have the work permit either, right?

Gennady: Yes, good point. Surprisingly quick thinking on your part, I must say.

work permit 취업 허가증

Dialogue 3

Vlad: Let's try to find a job first. The paperwork will only take a couple of days, anyway.

Gennady: Yes, you might be right. Let me grab a newspaper.

Vlad: In Russia we usually look for a job on the Internet. Don't you do the same here?

Gennady: The British may do so but I am a traditionalist. We need a newspaper with a good job section.

Vlad: But why would you need a newspaper? Everything is on the Internet.

Gennady: First the newspaper, then the Internet. Now, what have we got in here?

Vlad: Look at this one: "We offer a company car and a laptop, and a private office".

Gennady: Do they say anything about paid holidays or paid sick leave?

Vlad: No, they don't.

Gennady: Then leave it. Without a social package it's not worth considering.

paperwork 서류 작업 ㅣ **company car** 회사 차 ㅣ **office** 사무실 ㅣ **sick leave** 병가 ㅣ **social package** 사회 보장 제도

Vocabulary plus

broad	넓은	oral and written	구두와 서면의
clear objective	분명한 목표	out of one's league	~에게 어울리지 않는
climb up the career ladder	출세하다	pay slip	급여 명세서
communication	의사소통	qualified worker	유능한 직원
computer literate	컴퓨터에 밝은 사람	recruitment agency	인재 알선 업체
customer service	고객 서비스	remuneration	보수
develop	발전시키다	requirement	필요 조건, 자격
dream job	꿈의 직업	risk taker	모험적인 사람
fantasize	환상을 갖다	seeker	~을 추구하는 사람
field	분야	skill	기술
flexible working hours	탄력 근무제	social benefits	사회적 편익
Home Office	본사	software	소프트웨어
income tax	소득세	target-oriented	목표 지향적인
job security	고용 안정	team builder	팀을 꾸리는 사람
labour market	노동 시장	team player	단체 작업을 잘하는 사람
leadership	지도력	That's all there is to it.	그것이 전부이다.
managerial position	관리직	think forward	장래를 대비하다
nine-to-five job	오전 9시에 출근하여 5시에 퇴근하는 직업 (일반적인 사무직)	water current	물살
		well-organized	체계적인
on the spot	현장에서	white-collar job	사무직
on-the-job training	사내 훈련	working conditions	근무 환경

Cultural tips

Did you know that ...?

A **9-to-5 job** is a job with normal working hours, i.e. 9 a.m. to 5 p.m., Monday to Friday. In English-speaking countries, a **blue-collar worker**, in contrast to a white-collar worker, is a working-class person who performs manual jobs.

Scene 6 (30) Film dialogue and vocabulary

Read the dialogue between David (D) and Olive (O). Check the list of words and phrases below.

Lovely place, Olive. Do you stay here often?

Every time I'm in London ... They ask zero questions and the hourly rate is very affordable!

O: Now, show me your hand!
D: Ow! They may be broken! Ow! They are definitely broken!
O: No! Dislocated at most! ... Look, honey, we really need to talk about our relationship!
D: We do?
O: Yes, baby!
O: The big guy in the shop ... Judging by the accent, I'd say he might be Russian! A hitman, no doubt about it. He'll definitely kill us the moment he sees us again!
D: Don't you think we should talk to the police? We're in way over our heads!
O: David, your trust in the British police is ... touching. But I don't think they can protect us. Look, we could finish this tonight and disappear together!
D: Disappear together ... Leaving this whole mess behind us. Why can't we do this my way?

level B1

Vocabulary

zero	0, 영	Russian	러시아인
hourly rate	시간당 급료	hitman	청부 살인자
affordable	(가격) 알맞은	moment	순간
definitely	틀림없이	be in over one's head	~의 능력 밖이다
dislocated	탈구된	touching	감동적인
honey	자기 (부부, 애인 사이의 호칭)	protect	보호하다
relationship	관계	tonight	오늘밤
baby	자기 (부부, 애인 사이의 호칭)	disappear	사라지다
judge	판단하다	leave a mess	엉망으로 만들어 놓다
accent	강세	whole	전체

What should Olive do?

argue ⬇ B1-06-02

give up ⬇ B1-06-03

O: I'm a thief! I don't talk to the police. I run away from them!

D: And I'm a police constable. I make sure people who mess things up take responsibility for it! I need to think about it.

take responsibility for	~에 대한 책임을 지다

O: Fine! Let's call the police! If you really think it's the best option …

D: I need to think about it.

option	선택권

level B1 Scene 6 (30)

Grammar explanations

가능성을 나타내는 could, may/might

could — may/might — will — must
0% ———————————————————— 100%

could = 가능성이 매우 높은 경우

They **could** be anywhere now. 그들은 지금 어딘가에 있을 것입니다.
Mark **could** work as a taxi driver or a lorry driver. Mark는 택시 운전사나 트럭 운전사로 일하고 있을 것입니다.
I **could** buy it for you on my way home, if you want. 당신이 원한다면 제가 집에 오는 길에 그것을 사다 드릴 수 있습니다.

may/might = 가능성은 높지만 불확실한 경우

I **may/might** be home around 8 p.m. 저녁 8시쯤 저는 집에 있을 것입니다.
Peter **may/might** call you so take the phone with you.
Peter가 당신에게 전화를 할 수도 있으니 전화기를 가지고 가세요.
She **might** be a bit depressed after the exam. It was difficult for her.
시험 후 그녀는 약간 우울해 할 수도 있습니다. 그녀에게 어려웠어요.

→ could와 may/might는 대부분의 경우 교체 사용이 가능

  The weather **could/may/might** be nice tomorrow. 내일 날씨는 좋을 것입니다.
  They **could/may/might** come late. 그들은 늦게 올 것입니다.
  We **could/may/might** get lost without a map. 지도가 없으면 길을 잃을 것입니다.

확신의 의미를 나타내는 will, must

will = 경험에 바탕을 둔 가정

Don't touch the cat. It **will** scratch you! It's really afraid of strangers.
그 고양이는 건드리지 마세요. 당신을 할퀼 거예요! 낯선 사람을 매우 무서워하거든요.
Connie **will** remember the address. Her memory is excellent.
Connie가 주소를 기억할 거예요. 그녀의 기억력은 뛰어나거든요.
They **will** be at work now. It's only 2 p.m. and they don't finish until 5.
그들은 지금 일하고 있을 거예요. 이제 오후 2시인데, 5시까지는 일이 끝나지 않아요.

must = 예상을 근거로 한 확신

It **must** be mum. I have been waiting for her. 엄마임에 틀림없어요. 저는 엄마를 기다리고 있었어요.
I won't stay in this hotel. There **must** be a better place nearby.
저는 이 호텔에 묵지 않을 거예요. 근처에 분명 더 좋은 곳이 있을 거예요.
I keep calling her but there is no answer. She **must** be out of reach.
저는 그녀에게 계속 전화를 했지만 받지 않더군요. 그녀는 분명 통화 불능 지역에 있을 거예요.

가능성을 나타내는 can't/couldn't, may not/might not, won't

can't (cannot) = couldn't (could not) = 부정적 의미를 지닌 확신

It **can't** be Anna. She's not in the country. She's gone to Australia.
Anna일리가 없어요. 그녀는 이 나라에 없어요. 호주로 떠났어요.

You **can't** be serious! I don't believe you. 진담이 아니죠! 당신 말은 믿지 않아요.

She **couldn't** do it to me. We've got an agreement. 그녀가 제게 그럴 수는 없어요. 저희는 합의를 했거든요.

may not = might not (mightn't) = 가능성이 희박한 일에 대한 추측

They **may not** come today. I know they worked until late last night.
그들은 오늘 오지 못할 수도 있어요. 저는 그들이 어젯밤 늦게까지 일을 했다고 알고 있어요.

Sarah **might not** finish the marathon. She isn't as fit as she was last year.
Sarah는 마라톤을 완주하지 못할 수도 있어요. 그녀는 작년만큼 몸이 건강하지 않거든요.

We **mightn't** have time to see everything – Rome is full of great monuments from the past. 모든 것을 볼 수 있는 시간이 없을 수도 있어요 – 로마는 과거에 만들어진 멋진 기념물들로 가득하니까요.

won't (will not) = (경험에 근거한) 가능성이 희박한 일에 대한 추측

They **won't** lend you any money. They're too stingy.
그들은 당신에게 돈을 빌려 주지 않을 거예요. 그들은 너무 인색하거든요.

I can hear someone at the door! – It **won't** be any of your guests. It's too early.
문에서 누군가의 소리가 들려요! – 당신 손님은 아닐 거예요. 너무 이른 시간이잖아요.

Write the number down for me. I **won't** remember it otherwise.
저를 위해 숫자를 적어 주세요. 그렇지 않으면 제가 기억하지 못할 거예요.

level B1 Scene 6 (30)

Communication situations

Read the following dialogues between two friends meeting after a long time.

Beatrice? Is that you? Remember me? We went to the same school years ago.

Dialogue 1

Beatrice: Oh, what a surprise! How could I forget my first boyfriend? How are you?
Friend: Fine, thanks! But never mind me. Look at you! What a change!
Beatrice: It's been a while. People change, right?
Friend: Sure. So how's life? Are you married or single?
Beatrice: Actually, I'm single.
Friend: So am I. Maybe we shouldn't have broken up after all.
Beatrice: We did have some crazy times together, that's true.
Friend: Oh yes, we did. And why did we break up, actually?
Beatrice: Honestly? I can't remember now.
Friend: Neither can I. So it couldn't have been something serious. How about a drink then?
Beatrice: No. You don't step into the same river twice.
Friend: Oh please, it's just a drink. For old times' sake.

For old times' sake. 옛정을 생각해서.

Dialogue 2

Beatrice: Yes, I remember you.

Friend: Erm ... So, how are you? I have to say you look stunning!

Beatrice: Thanks. Sorry, but I don't feel like talking to you.

Friend: All right. May I ask why?

Beatrice: I don't have good memories about you from our school days.

Friend: Oh, right. I wasn't very kind to you then. Maybe we could clear that up over a cup of coffee?

Beatrice: No, I don't think so.

Friend: OK. I understand. Well, it was nice seeing you again. Take care! Bye!

feel like (doing something) ~하고 싶다 | **clear up** 정리하다 | **Take care!** 잘 지내!

Dialogue 3

Beatrice: Oh, what a surprise! How could I forget my first boyfriend? How are you?

Friend: Fine, thanks! But never mind me. Look at you! What a change!

Beatrice: Well, yes. It's because of my job, you know.

Friend: I remember you wanted to become a full time eco-activist. But I'm guessing you're not one, right?

Beatrice: No, that was a childish dream. I'm a soldier.

Friend: Excuse me? Are you kidding me?

Beatrice: Well, I'm not in a uniform right now but yes, I'm a soldier.

Friend: How did that happen?

Beatrice: Well, I have always been a rebel, remember?

Friend: Yes! But you rebelled against the system, not in favour of it!

Beatrice: When we broke up, things changed.

Friend: Don't tell me you became a soldier because of me!

Beatrice: No. It was partly because of that scholarship I got.

Friend: Oh, I knew that scholarship was a bad idea. Just kidding! How about you telling me all about it over a drink? My treat. If you don't mind, of course.

childish 어린애 같은 | **soldier** 군인 | **rebel** 반대자, 반항아 | **in favour of** ~에 찬성하여 | **partly** 부분적으로 | **My treat.** 내가 살게.

Vocabulary plus

apologise	사과하다
biker	오토바이 혹은 자전거를 타는 사람
bump into	~와 마주치다
by sight	얼굴은, 안면으로
chippy	튀김 음식 전문점
condescending	잘난 체하는
Congratulations!	축하합니다!
divorced	이혼한
get to know	알게 되다
grant	보조금
Have it your way.	좋을 대로 하세요.
I don't fancy ...	~을 원하지 않다
I had the time of my life.	그때가 최고였어요.
keep under wraps	~을 비밀로 하다
memory	기억
mixed	혼성의
modelling	모델 일
relief	안도
saying	속담, 격언
settle down	정착하다
swap stories	이야기를 나누다
Thanks, but no thanks.	고맙지만 사양하겠습니다.
whirlwind romance	정신없이 벌어진 연애

Cultural tips

Did you know that …?

999 is the official emergency telephone number in a number of countries, including the UK and Ireland, which allows the caller to contact emergency services in the case of an accident.

Scene 7 (31) — Film dialogue and vocabulary

Read the dialogue between Vlad (V), Sergey (S) and David (D). Check the list of words and phrases below.

Remember! No killing! Just like my father told you!

You stay here!

V: What?

S: What do you mean "what"? When I took this job, I'd discussed the issue of violence with my father. He said he had already explained it to you that we're supposed to … you're supposed to rough them up a bit, take what's stolen and that's it! Is that correct?

V: He told you … that?

S: He made a promise!

V: Okay, I'll see what I can do! You … watch my back! If something … happens, use that gun!

D: And I'm going to say … Olive, it's time for you to make up your … Oh shit!

Vocabulary			
discuss	의논하다	explain	설명하다
issue	문제	rough up	두들겨 패다
violence	폭력	be correct	정확하다

level **B1**

David returns to the hotel and meets Sergey in the hall. What should David do?

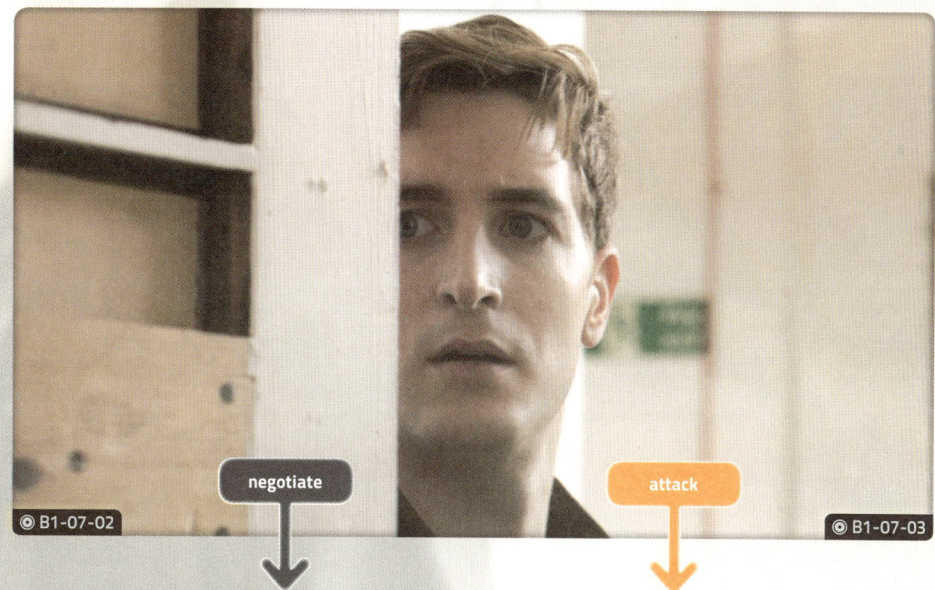

negotiate ◎ B1-07-02

attack ◎ B1-07-03

D: Look, I'm not going to hurt you, okay? You see that? I'm a police officer! I need you to put the gun down!

S: This pistol ... I don't even know how to ... (...) Vlad! Help!

S: Oh! ... Not again, please!

| pistol | 권총 |

Game over.
Try again.

level B1 Scene 7 (31)   61

Grammar explanations

과거완료

→ 과거의 동작 전에 일어난 활동이나 사건을 나타낸다.
I/you/he/she/it/we/they + **had ('d)** + 과거분사

I **had studied** English before I started to work in the UK.
저는 영국에서 일을 시작하기 전에 영어를 배웠습니다.

We **had read** 3 books about Rome before we went to Italy.
저희는 이탈리아로 가기 전에 로마에 관한 책을 3권 읽었습니다.

The film **had started** when we arrived at the cinema.
우리가 영화관에 도착했을 때 영화는 시작을 했습니다.

Everybody **had already left** when I came.
제가 도착했을 때 이미 모두 떠났습니다.

→ **before, after, when, already**와 함께 사용

−	I/you/he/she/it/we/they + **hadn't (had not)** + 과거분사 We **hadn't solved** the problem before we gathered all the data. 모든 자료를 수집하기 전에는 문제를 해결할 수 없었습니다.
?	**Had** + I/you/he/she/it/we/they + 과거분사 **Had** you **been** in the USA before you came to study there? 미국으로 공부하러 오기 전에 미국에 왔던 적이 있나요?
+/−	Yes, I/you/he/she/it/we/they **had**. No, I/you/he/she/it/we/they **hadn't (had not)**. **Had** you **been** there before? – Yes, I **had**. 전에 그곳에 가 본 적이 있었나요? – 네, 있었어요. **Had** she **sung** that song before? – No, she **hadn't (had not)**. 그녀가 전에 그 노래를 부른 적이 있었나요? – 아니요, 없었어요.

과거완료 vs. 과거

과거완료	과거
→ 과거의 특정한 시점 전에 일어난 사건 When I came home, the news **had started**. I missed the beginning. 집에 왔을 때 뉴스가 시작되었습니다. 처음 부분은 놓쳤습니다. after, before, when, already와 어울림	→ 과거의 일시적인 행동이나 사건 혹은 연대순의 행동이나 사건 When I **came** home, the news **started**. I was just in time for the beginning. 집에 왔을 때 뉴스가 시작되었습니다. 시간에 딱 맞게 와서 처음 부분을 볼 수 있었습니다. when과 어울림

Communication situations

Read the following dialogues. Olive and her psychologist are talking about her emotions and feelings.

Hello Olive, come in. You are earlier than usual today. I can see your eyes are red and swollen. Were those tears of joy or sadness? What has happened, Olive?

Dialogue 1

Olive: Yes, I have been crying a lot since yesterday. I'm hopeless.

Psychologist: Don't be so hard on yourself. Come on, have a seat. Here is some water. Now, what's happened?

Olive: Yesterday I was criticized by a person whose opinion means a lot to me.

Psychologist: And how did you react?

Olive: I immediately got upset. Actually, I was furious.

Psychologist: What made you furious?

Olive: My employer said I let him down.

Psychologist: How did you feel when you heard that?

Olive: Like a schoolgirl who hadn't done her homework.

Psychologist: Your employer became your teacher. And you lost faith in yourself. We can't let that happen again.

---

cry 울다 | hopeless 절망적인 | have a seat 앉다 | react 반응하다 | immediately 즉시 | furious 분노한 | employer 고용주 | let somebody down ~을 실망시키다 | faith 신뢰

Dialogue 2

Olive: Yes, I have cried, but with joy!

Psychologist: That's good news. What happened?

Olive: I finally stole the Mona Lisa yesterday!

Psychologist: What?! Don't say a word! I don't want to be questioned by the police when they come after you!

Olive: Oh, come on. I'm so excited!

Psychologist: I bet you are but I've got mixed feelings about it, to put it mildly.

Olive: Don't spoil it. I'm over the moon.

Psychologist: Yes. And I'm scared stiff.

---

joy 즐거움 | news 소식 | question 심문하다 | to put it mildly 조심스럽게 말하면 | be over the moon 매우 기쁘다 | scared stiff 겁에 질려 몸이 굳은

Dialogue 3

Olive: It's my colleague. He drives me crazy.

Psychologist: All right. I won't ask about the reason for your anger.
Let's be productive and focus on the way of coping with it.

Olive: No, we have talked about that already.

Psychologist: Indeed, but you don't seem as stable as I could wish.

Olive: There is so much hatred in me.

Psychologist: All right, I see. So we'll end up talking about you eventually. That's fine.

---

anger 분노 | productive 생산적인 | cope with 대처하다 | stable 안정적인

Vocabulary plus

be up to somebody	~에게 달려 있다	gut feeling	직감
born under a lucky star	행운을 타고난	Hold your horses.	침착하세요.
		improper	부당한
burn out	에너지를 소진하다	in somebody's shoes	~의 입장에서
burst into tears	울음이 터지다	in the short run	단기적으로
burst out laughing	웃음이 터지다	jail	감옥
challenge	도전	lose one's temper	버럭 화를 내다
come to an end	끝나다	mentally	정신적으로
confident	자신감 있는	mood swings	감정 기복
counterproductive	역효과를 낳는	petrified	겁에 질린
face	직면하다	reflect	반사하다
feel relieved	안도하다	sadness	슬픔
find the way out	탈출구를 찾다	self-esteem	자부심
get down	우울하게 하다	supportive	지원하는
get on somebody's nerves	~의 심기를 건들다	undermine	약화시키다
		unreliable	신뢰할 수 없는
go with the flow	흐름에 맡기다		
goal	목표		

Cultural tips

Did you know that ...?

The "ER" symbol on police badges in the UK stands for Elizabeth Regina (Queen Elizabeth II in Latin). It is a royal cypher used to identify the queen and stamp Her Majesty's identity. These small initials are often seen in place of the queen's full name and title.

Scene 8 (32) — Film dialogue and vocabulary

Read Vlad's monologue. Check the list of words and phrases below.

I thought you should finish … washing your hair.

I … remember nice hair … was important for my wife, too! She was bigger than you … tall, beautiful, proud woman. Strong as … er … an ox! Sometimes … she got angry with me, I was afraid. Fatter here … much fatter … But her eyes … Like yours! (…) I … removed the bullets from that one, so no shooting, huh? Now you give me the documents, yes?

Vocabulary

wash	씻다	get angry with	노하다
hair	머리	be afraid of	~을 두려워하다
tall	키가 큰	fat	뚱뚱한
beautiful	아름다운	eye	눈
strong as an ox	아주 튼튼한	bullet	총알

level B1

Read the dialogue between David (D), Sergey (S) and Vlad (V). Check the list of words and phrases below.

S: He's a psychotic, unstoppable killing machine! If you start fighting, we're all going to die!

D: Shut up or I'll punch you once again!

V: See, Sergey? I've just … r-o-u-g-h-e-d her up a bit! But she is fit as a … fiddle.

Vocabulary			
psychotic	정신병 환자	punch	주먹으로 치다
unstoppable	막을 수 없는	fit as a fiddle	매우 건강한
machine	기계		

Grammar explanations

다양한 형용사들

1. 의견	2. 크기/길이	3. 연령/시대	4. 모양
nice, fantastic, wonderful, terrible, awful, great, beautiful	big, small, large, enormous, short, tall, tiny	new, old, young, ancient	oval, square, round, rectangular, flat, curly, straight
5. 색상	6. 출신	7. 재료	8. 목적/용도
red, blue, white, black, yellow, reddish, yellowish, green, golden	American, British, European, Roman, eastern, northern	plastic, leather, paper, wooden, cotton, gold, silk	sleeping (bag), electric (kettle), bath (towel), kitchen (knife), doctor's, John's, the Smiths'

형용사 어미 –ed와 –ing

동사(annoy, confuse, terrify, worry 등)에서 파생된 형용사

-ed

➜ 사람의 감정 묘사

I was **annoyed** by their behaviour.
저는 그들의 행동에 화가 났어요. (동사 annoy)

She felt **confused** when she heard the news.
그녀는 뉴스를 듣고 혼란스러워 했어요. (동사 confuse)

We were **disappointed** by the result of the meeting.
우리는 회의 결과에 실망했어요. (동사 disappoint)

-ing

➜ 사물 혹은 상황 묘사

Their behaviour was **annoying**.
그들의 행동은 성가신 것이었어요. (동사 annoy)

The news was **confusing**.
그 뉴스는 혼란스러운 것이었어요. (동사 confuse)

The result of the meeting was **disappointing**.
회의 결과는 실망스러웠어요. (동사 disappoint)

Communication situations

Read the following phone dialogues. Olive and David are talking about their Christmas shopping.

> Hi love, what's up? Have you found everything from the list?

Dialogue 1

David: No, and it's the last time I'm doing our Christmas shopping!

Olive: OK, fine. Please find the section with the Christmas decorations and gather the things from the list one by one.

David: All right. Lighting stuff. What exactly are we looking for this year?

Olive: Some decorative lights for the living room.

David: This one is beautiful. An eight-pointed white steel star. With built-in LED lights, of course.

Olive: Oh, it may look nice over the Christmas tree. Buy it.

Christmas tree 크리스마스 트리 | gather 모으다 | lights 조명 | steel 쇠로 된

Dialogue 2

David: No. That's why I'm calling. I'm in the furnishing shop.

Olive: OK, fine. Please find the section with the Christmas decorations and gather the things from the list one by one.

David: OK. Decoration department. Oh, there are some really nice pieces here.

Olive: Remember, we are looking for something in red and gold. What can you see?

David: Gold? I'm as good as gold.

Olive: I know, sweetheart. But I can't hang you on a Christmas tree, can I?

David: OK. Shall I look for something wooden, paper or plastic?

Olive: The material is not that important. Concentrate on the look.

David: There are some small, wooden, red and white snowflakes here. Very pretty. Interested?

Olive: Yes. As long as you find them in red and gold, that is.

furnishing shop 실내 장식 용품점 | **gold** 금 | **hang** 매달다 | **snowflake** 눈송이 | **wooden** 목재의

Dialogue 3

David: You must be joking! I'm in the toy shop. Everything looks the same here.

Olive: That's impossible. Take a deep breath and really look around.

David: Everything is either baby pink or baby blue. And so candy coloured it makes my teeth hurt.

Olive: Well, it's a shop for children. What do you expect?

David: It's really confusing. I don't know where to go now.

Olive: You are going to buy a doll for a girl, so go to the pink part now and tell me what you see.

David: OK, I'm here. Oh God, I've never seen so many dolls in one place …

Olive: Easy love, don't get too excited. Just pick one up and describe it to me.

David: It's nice to the touch. A bit fluffy and with curly brown hair.

Olive: Are you sure it's not a teddy bear?

David: Give me some credit, love. I didn't play with cars only when I was little.

Olive: All right. If you like it, take it.

David: Good. One aisle is done.

Olive: See? You'll be done with it all in no time.

toy shop 장난감 가게 | **candy coloured** 알록달록한 | **confusing** 혼란스러운 | **doll** 인형 | **place** 장소; ~에 두다 | **pick** 집다 | **describe** 묘사하다 | **nice to the touch** 촉감이 좋은 | **fluffy** 푹신한 | **curly** 곱슬거리는 | **teddy bear** 테디베어 | **play** 놀다

Vocabulary plus

atrocity	잔혹 행위	paint	페인트
bauble	(겉만 화려한) 값싼 물건	porch	현관
belly	배	princess	공주
cage	우리	put back	제자리에 갖다 놓다
chiefly	주로	rag doll	헝겊 인형
cotton	면	reindeer	순록
dozen	12개	search	찾아보다
fresh	신선한	shop assistant	점원
garland	화환	simplicity	간단함
grumpy	기분이 언짢은	sleigh	썰매
keep on (doing something)	계속 ~하다	toddler	걸음마를 배우는 아이
		waist	허리
needles	솔잎	wreath	화환

Cultural tips

Did you know that …?

A teddy bear is a soft children's toy in the form of a bear. It was developed at the same time in the U.S. and in Germany in the early 20th century. It is named after President Theodore Roosevelt, who was commonly known as "Teddy" (but he hated being called that).

Scene 9 (33)   Film dialogue and vocabulary

Read the dialogue between Vlad (V), David (D) and Olive (O). Check the list of words below.

V: You are going to do that? Really? ... No! You're frightened! ... No idea what you're doing!

D: I do know what I'm doing!

V: Look, we need the documents ... but I don't have to kill you. No! Sergey, tell him! We don't have to kill them, do we? Just give me the documents you stole! And there's no problem! Everyone happy! Yes?

O: David, don't give them to him!

frightened	겁먹은	everyone	모든 사람

What should David do?

O: Why did you do that? Why?

V: Why? ... To protect you, stupid girl! Sorry!

D: No, you're lying!

V: I am! All right, let's get ... down to it!

S: What are you doing, Vlad?

V: What your father told me to do! ... David, your last chance!

D: Okay then, let the killing begin! Why don't we start with this guy! I can't stand him!

S: No, no! Don't do that, please!

V: Stop! Don't shoot! ... Please! Can't do this to your father, Sergey! You're his only child!

chance	기회
begin	시작하다

Grammar explanations

관계대명사

관계대명사 + 전치사 = 전치사 + 관계대명사

cf.「전치사 + 관계대명사」형태가 보다 정중한 표현

who

The person **who** I rely **on** the most is David. 제가 가장 많이 의지하는 사람은 David입니다.
= The person **on whom** I rely the most is David. (on who (×))

whom

Gennady's son, Sergey, is the man **whom** Vlad came **with**. Gennady의 아들 Sergey는 Vlad와 함께 온 사람입니다.
= Gennady's son, Sergey, is the man **with whom** Vlad came.

which

Thistle Flowers is the painting **which** Olive was interested **in**. '엉겅퀴 꽃'은 Olive가 관심을 가졌던 그림입니다.
= Thistle Flowers is the painting **in which** Olive was interested.

시간과 장소를 나타내는 관계대명사와 관계부사

전치사 + which = 관계부사

on/in which (시간) ➜ when

I remember the day **on which** Kennedy was shot. 저는 Kennedy가 총격을 당한 날을 기억합니다.
= I remember the day **when** Kennedy was shot.

April is the month **in which** the buds begin to open. 4월은 꽃봉오리가 열리기 시작하는 달입니다.
= April is the month **when** the buds begin to open.

at/in/to which (장소) ➜ where

It was the strangest restaurant **at which** we have ever eaten.
그곳은 우리가 식사를 했던 곳 중에서 가장 특이한 식당이었습니다.
= It was the strangest restaurant **where** we have ever eaten.

The room **in which** he keeps his priceless collection has no windows.
그가 귀중한 수집품을 보관해 놓는 방에는 창문이 없습니다.
= The room **where** he keeps his priceless collection has no windows.

They could already see the village **to which** they were going.
그들은 자신들이 가게 될 마을을 미리 볼 수 있었습니다.
= They could already see the village **where** they were going.

관계대명사의 격

The two men who were following Olive and David worked for Robert Murray.

Olive와 David를 뒤쫓고 있던 두 남자는 Robert Murray를 위해 일하는 사람이었습니다. (주격)

Robert had **the documents that** Olive stole. = **Robert** had **the documents** Olive stole.

Robert는 Olive가 훔친 문서를 가지고 있었습니다. (목적격)

➜ 주격 관계대명사와 달리 목적격 관계대명사는 생략이 가능

I don't remember **the name of the company** (**which**) I worked for 5 years ago.
저는 5년 전에 다녔던 회사의 이름이 기억나지 않습니다.

She likes **the coat** (**that**) **she** bought last autumn.
그녀는 지난 가을에 구입한 코트를 좋아합니다.

Communication situations

Read the following dialogues between a mother and her daughter who reads unusual books on the day before an exam.

> Hi, I've just popped in to say hello and check how you are doing the day before your exam. I guess you must be doing fine since you are not at your desk.

Dialogue 1

Daughter: Come on, lying on a bed doesn't mean I'm not nervous or unprepared for the exam.

Mother: Quite the contrary. It only proves you are well prepared.

Daughter: Exactly. Finally somebody with a clear head.

Mother: Brilliant! And I can see you are reading something.

Daughter: Yes. It is a chick lit book.

Mother: Chick lit? Shame on you.

Daughter: Why? I think there is potential in it.

Mother: You are joking, aren't you?

Daughter: No, I'm not. Just listen: Once upon a time …

Mother: Stop. I know the ending. And they lived happily ever after …

---

unprepared 준비되지 않은 | **prove** 증명하다 | **clear head** 명석한 두뇌 | **chick lit** 여자들 소설 | **Shame on you!** 부끄러운 줄 알아라! | **Once upon a time** 옛날 옛적에 | **ending** 결말 | **And they lived happily ever after.** 그리고 그 후 그들은 행복하게 살았습니다.

Dialogue 2

Daughter: Yeah, I'm fine. Well prepared. It's time to relax.

Mother: Let me see what you are reading. Hmm. "Top 10 Most Hilarious Stories of the Year". Tell me about the one you are reading now.

Daughter: It's a story about a dead kangaroo.

Mother: It sounds intriguing. Tell me about it.

Daughter: Well, a sailor stopped by the coast of Australia during the America's Cup yacht race.

Mother: And ...?

Daughter: One day he went for a drive. He was driving fast when he felt he'd bumped into something.

Mother: And that was the kangaroo.

Daughter: Yes. Apparently the kangaroo was knocked out.

Mother: Oh no! Poor thing! What happened next?

Daughter: When the kangaroo woke up a minute later, it was wearing the sailor's jacket.

Mother: Did the kangaroo like it?

Daughter: How can I know that?

Mother: So what's the point?

Daughter: They both ended up with a useless thing.

Mother: Aha. And is that what makes you laugh?

---

hilarious 재미있는 | **intriguing** 복잡한 | **sailor** 선원 | **drive** 드라이브 | **knock out** 기절시키다 | **poor thing** 불쌍한 것 | **useless** 쓸모 없는 | **make laugh** 웃게 하다

Vocabulary plus

academic	학업의
approach	~에 접근하다
bloody	피의
bug	벌레
coincidence	우연의 일치
costly	많은 비용이 드는
cover	충당하다
cut a long story short	간단히 줄여서 말하면
dress up	변장하다
get into	~에 들어가다
go off	폭발하다
go through	겪다
insect repellent	방충제
inside	안쪽에서
line	줄
mind-numbing	정신이 멍해질 만큼의
misunderstanding	오해
Now I get it!	이제 알겠어요!
out of the blue	난데없이
parking lot	주차장
plant	~을 몰래 장치하다
point at	가리키다
quite some lady	대단한 여자
rent	임대하다
run over	(차로) 치다
security	경비
seemingly	겉보기에
take for	간주하다
take the exam	시험을 치르다
threaten	위협하다
unwind	긴장을 풀다
Who cares?	알 게 뭐야?

Cultural tips

Did you know that …?

A nuclear family is a family unit consisting of a pair of adults and their children (any number of them). A nuclear family is a part of an extended family, which also includes aunts, uncles, cousins, grandparents etc.

Scene 10 (34)   Film dialogue and vocabulary

Read the dialogue between Olive (O) and Vlad (V). Check the list of phrases below.

We're taking your friend for a ride! … So, I don't want to see you following us!

You will! I'll be after you in no time!

| take for a ride | 태워주다 |

Read the dialogue between David (D), Olive (O) and Sergey (S). Check the list of words and phrases below.

What is that?

It's the door being broken down.

S: He said he'd be after you in no time! But I can still change his mind if you just let me … This doesn't have to end with people dying!

O: David! … You're about to go for a ride!

S: Please, no! I'll tell you how we found you!

O: How?

S: The guy whose documents you stole gave him a mobile phone that we can track. He asked my father to find you, retrieve the stuff, and apparently, also to kill you!

| mobile (phone) | 휴대폰 | retrieve | 되찾아오다 |
| track | 추적하다 | apparently | 분명히 |

Grammar explanations

간접화법

I said: "I will come back late." 저는 "나중에 돌아올게요."라고 말했습니다. (직접화법)
I said I would come back late. 저는 나중에 돌아오겠다고 말했습니다. (간접화법)

The teacher said: "I have been waiting for you." 선생님께서는 "너희들을 기다리고 있을게."라고 말씀하셨습니다. (직접화법)
The teacher said she had been waiting for us. 선생님께서는 저희를 기다리고 있겠다고 말씀하셨습니다. (간접화법)

Tom said: "I don't smoke." Tom은 "저는 담배를 피우지 않아요."라고 말했습니다. (직접화법)
He said he didn't smoke. Tom은 자신이 담배를 피우지 않는다고 말했습니다. (간접화법)

You said: "It may be a good idea." 당신은 "좋은 아이디어일 수도 있겠군요."라고 말했습니다. (직접화법)
You said it might be a good idea. 당신은 좋은 아이디어일 수도 있겠다고 말했습니다. (간접화법)

간접화법에서의 시제 변화

현재 ➡ 과거
I said: "I am busy now." 저는 "지금 매우 바쁩니다."라고 말했습니다. (직접화법)
I said I was busy. 저는 매우 바쁘다고 말했습니다. (간접화법)

현재진행 ➡ 과거진행
She said: "I am cooking dinner." 그녀는 "저녁을 요리하는 중이에요."라고 말했습니다. (직접화법)
She said she was cooking dinner. 그녀는 저녁을 요리하는 중이라고 말했습니다. (간접화법)

현재완료 ➡ 과거완료
They said: "We have known each other for 5 years." 그들은 "우리는 5년간 서로를 알고 지냈어요."라고 말했습니다. (직접화법)
They said they had known each other for 5 years. 그들은 5년간 서로를 알고 지냈다고 말했습니다. (간접화법)

현재완료진행 ➡ 과거완료진행
She said: "I have been working in the garden." 그녀는 "정원에서 일을 하고 있었어요."라고 말했습니다. (직접화법)
She said she had been working in the garden. 그녀는 정원에서 일을 하고 있었다고 말했습니다. (간접화법)

과거 ➡ 과거완료
She said: "I baked the cake especially for you." 그녀는 "당신을 위해 특별히 케이크를 만들었어요."라고 말했습니다. (직접화법)
She said she had baked the cake especially for me. 그녀는 저를 위해 특별히 케이크를 만들었다고 말했습니다. (간접화법)

과거진행 ➡ 과거완료진행

He said: "I was repairing my car the whole afternoon." 그는 "저는 오후 내내 차를 고치고 있었어요."라고 말했습니다. (직접화법)

He said he had been repairing his car the whole afternoon. 그는 자신이 오후 내내 차를 고치고 있었다고 말했습니다. (간접화법)

과거완료 ➡ 과거완료

I said: "I had visited that place many times before 2012." 저는 "2012년 전에 그곳을 여러 번 방문한 적이 있어요."라고 말했습니다. (직접화법)

I said I had visited that place many times before 2012. 저는 2012년 전에 그곳을 여러 번 방문한 적이 있다고 말했습니다. (간접화법)

미래 ➡ would

He said: "I will come back soon." 그는 "곧 돌아올게요."라고 말했습니다. (직접화법)

He said he would come back soon. 그는 곧 돌아오겠다고 말했습니다. (간접화법)

간접화법에서의 인칭 변화

Tom said: "I am enjoying your party".
Tom은 "당신의 파티를 즐기고 있어요."라고 말했습니다.

⬇

Tom said he was enjoying my party.
Tom은 저의 파티를 즐기고 있다고 말했습니다.

Teresa said: "I had a lovely weekend."
Teresa는 "저는 멋진 주말을 보냈어요."라고 말했습니다.

⬇

Teresa said she had had a lovely weekend.
Teresa는 멋진 주말을 보냈다고 말했습니다.

Remember!
간접화법에서 대명사는 내용에 맞게 변경되어야 한다.

You said: "I will take care of your garden while you are away."
당신은 "당신이 나가 있는 동안에 당신의 정원을 가꿀 거예요."라고 말했습니다.

⬇

You said you would take care of my garden while I was away.
당신은 제가 나가 있는 동안 저의 정원을 가꿀 것이라고 말했습니다.

간접화법과 부정문

과거 시제의 be동사의 부정형

Mary said: "I **am not** afraid of flying." Mary는 "저는 비행이 두렵지 않아요."라고 말했습니다.
Mary said she **wasn't** afraid of flying. Mary는 비행이 두렵지 않다고 말했습니다.

과거 시제의 부정형

We said: "We **don't like** the party."
저희는 "파티를 좋아하지 않아요."라고 말했습니다.
We said we **didn't like** the party.
저희는 파티를 좋아하지 않는다고 말했습니다.

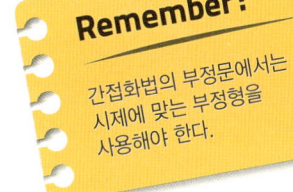

Remember!
간접화법의 부정문에서는 시제에 맞는 부정형을 사용해야 한다.

과거완료의 부정형

They said: "We **didn't miss** the bus." 그들은 "우리는 버스를 놓치지 않았어요."라고 말했습니다.
They said they **hadn't missed** the bus. 그들은 자신들이 버스를 놓치지 않았다고 말했습니다.

would의 부정형

I said: "I **will not** visit her again." 저는 "그녀를 다시 방문하지 않겠어요."라고 말했습니다.
I said I **wouldn't** visit her again. 저는 그녀를 다시 방문하지 않겠다고 말했습니다.

간접화법과 의문문

➔ 일반 의문문: (she) asked if/whether ...

Are you hungry? – **No**, I'm **not**. 배가 고픈가요? – 아니요, 그렇지 않아요.
He asked: "**Are** you hungry?" 그는 "배가 고픈가요?"라고 물었습니다.
He asked **if** I **was** hungry. 그는 저에게 배가 고픈지 물었습니다.

Were you satisfied with the result? – **Yes**, I **was**. 결과에 만족했나요? – 네, 그랬어요.
She asked me: "**Were** you satisfied with the result?" 그녀는 제게 "결과에 만족했나요?"라고 물었습니다.
She asked me **whether** I **had been** satisfied with the result. 그녀는 제게 결과에 만족했는지 물었습니다.

➔ 의문사 의문문: (she) asked when/where/who/how/why + 적절한 시제

Where were you last night? – Yesterday I was on a business trip.
어젯밤에 어디에 있었니? – 어제 출장 중이었어.
A friend asked me: "**Where were you** last night?" 한 친구가 제게 "어젯밤에 어디에 있었니?"라고 물었습니다.
A friend asked me **where I had been** last night. 한 친구가 제게 어젯밤에 어디에 있었는지 물었습니다.

When are you going to bake the cake? – I think the night before would be fine.
언제 빵을 구울 건가요? – 그 전날 밤이면 좋을 것 같아요.
She asked: "**When are you going to** bake the cake?" 그녀는 "언제 빵을 구울 건가요?"라고 물었습니다.
She asked **when we were going to** bake the cake. 그녀는 언제 빵을 구울 것인지 물었습니다.

Communication situations

Read the following dialogues. Olive and David are waiting for their flight at an airport in France.

... and then I will turn my mobile off, take a hot shower and sleep as long as I can!

Dialogue 1

David: Wait! Have you heard the announcement?

Olive: I don't know, your French is better than mine. What did they say?

David: I think the plane is delayed.

Olive: And now what?

David: Now we have to find out how big the delay is.

Olive: Let's hope it's just a few hours and not a full day.

David: In case it takes a day or more the airlines will provide us with accommodation.

Olive: Whatever! I want to start our holiday already! We've waited so long and now this …

---

announcement 소식 | **plane** 비행기 | **delay** 지연, 지연시키다 | **full** 완전한; 가득 찬 | **airline** 항공사 | **accommodation** 숙박 시설

Dialogue 2

David: One moment. I think there has been a change.

Olive: Oops, sorry! Can't they repeat it?

David: Wait a moment. I'll go to the information desk and ask for details.

(…)

Olive: And what did the lady say?

David: Due to dense fog we won't fly today.

Olive: OK. I'm sure we are not the only ones stranded here. Have you asked her about a transfer?

David: No, I haven't. I'll go back and ask. Any other suggestions?

Olive: Ask about the luggage. Shall we wait for it or not?

David: It's a good thing you're a frequent flyer.

Olive: And you know French! It's a match made in heaven, isn't it? Now, go and ask her, so we can decide what to do next.

---

dense 짙은 | **fog** 안개 | **information desk** 안내 데스크 | **stranded** 발 묶인, 고립된 | **transfer** 환승; 전근 | **a frequent flyer** 상용 고객 | **match made in heaven** 천생연분, 찰떡궁합

Dialogue 3

David: Shh! Haven't they said something about our plane?

Olive: I don't know, your French is better than mine. What did they say?

David: I think we are supposed to proceed to the gate.

Olive: To the gate? But we haven't checked in yet!

David: We did the checking-in online. Don't you remember?

Olive: Oh, right! What a relief! So what was that about the gate?

David: They said it's open and the boarding has started.

Olive: Already? That's a bit too soon. I wanted to go to the duty-free shop first!

---

gate (공항) 게이트 | **board** 탑승하다; (역·공항의) 게시판 | **boarding** 탑승 | **duty-free** 면세의

Vocabulary plus

be used to	~에 익숙하다	pay off	(결실) 맺다
cancelled	취소된	rental	대여
check in	(공항의) 탑승수속을 하다	repetition	반복
French speaker	불어 사용자	So long!	안녕 (작별 인사)
frustrating	좌절감을 주는	spare time	여가 시간
get one's knickers in a twist	당황하다	switch	바꾸다
		uncalled for	부적절한
have to do with	~와 관계가 있다	updated	갱신된
impractical	비효율적인	vacation	휴가
land	착륙하다		

Cultural tips

Did you know that …?

British Airways (BA) is the largest airline in the United Kingdom based on fleet size. The airline is based in Waterside near its main hub at London Heathrow Airport.

American Airlines (AA) is the largest airline in the United States based on fleet size. The airline is based in Texas and has several hubs across the U.S.

Scene 11 (35)   Film dialogue and vocabulary

Read the dialogue between Olive (O) and David (D). Check the list of words and phrases below.

D: Okay, maybe I am working for Murray, but he blackmailed me into this! I was about to tell you ... but the Russian guys came and I just ...

O: Blackmailed you? Is this why you wanted to find me?

D: No! I wanted to find you because I care for you! Why is it obvious to a Russian thug, but not to you!

O: I'm to deliver the documents to my client this evening. For the time being, this is all that matters. And you ... I thought your presence would make it easier for me, but no! You're distracting me, and making me vulnerable ... I can't be like that! This transaction has to take place tonight!

D: Does it? Because of the money you'll get?

O: No! You're not the only person being blackmailed here. I also need to protect the people I care for. And that includes ... you!

D: You know, I was on the point of giving up on my previous life. But too many people can get hurt because of what we're doing. ... I'll tell Murray to leave you alone. If not, I'll go to the press with this thing ... whatever it is.

level B1

You probably hate me right now, but if one day you feel like giving us a second chance ...

Vocabulary

blackmail	협박하다	vulnerable	취약한, 연약한
obvious	명백한	include	포함하다
thug	폭력배	previous	이전의
matter	중요하다	the press	언론
presence	존재	whatever	무엇이든지
distract	집중이 안 되게 하다		

Grammar explanations

미래를 나타내는 be to와 be about to

be to + 동사 원형

→ 공식적인 계획

The Queen **is to visit** Canada in September. 여왕께서 9월에 캐나다를 방문하실 것입니다.

→ 과거에 일어나지 않은 사건

The meeting with the officials **was to take place** after the ceremony but due to a delay it was cancelled. 의식이 끝난 후 공무원과의 회의가 예정되어 있었지만 연착 때문에 회의가 취소되었습니다.

be about to + 동사 원형

→ 매우 가까운 미래의 행동

I'**m about to leave**. 저는 이제 막 떠나려던 참이었어요.
= I'm leaving in a minute or so.

→ 과거에 일어나지 않은 사건

I **was about to tell** you but the Russian guys came. 당신에게 말하려던 참이었는데 러시아 사람들이 왔어요.
= I was going to tell you in that moment when the Russian guys came.

미래를 나타내는 be on the point of / be on the verge of / be on the edge of

to be on the point of + -ing
to be on the verge of + -ing = to be about to + 동사 원형
to be on the edge of + -ing

I **was on the point of** giv**ing** up my previous life.
저는 저의 예전 삶을 포기하려던 참이었어요.

She **is on the verge of** mov**ing** to Australia for good.
그녀는 호주로 영원히 떠날 참이었어요.

He **is on the edge of** mak**ing** the biggest mistake in his life.
그는 인생에서 가장 큰 실수를 할 뻔 했어요.

Remember!

이러한 구문들이 과거시제로 사용되는 경우에는 과거에 일어나지 않은 사건을 나타낸다. Robert **was on the edge of** disclosing why Olive had come to Old Berry. Robert는 Olive가 왜 Old Berry에 왔는지 밝히려고 했습니다. (하지만 밝히지 못함)

Communication situations

Read the following dialogues between friends talking about social media and the information available on the Internet.

Hello! Earth to Beatrice! Can you hear me? Why are you staring into space like that?

Dialogue 1

Beatrice: Oh sorry. I was lost in thought.

Friend: I can see that. What's the reason?

Beatrice: Let me ask you something first. Do you use social media?

Friend: Well, of course I'm online. Everybody is.

Beatrice: Well, that's the problem. I'm not.

Friend: Then you should get down to it, unless you want to become invisible.

Beatrice: I don't feel like sharing my life with so called "friends" that I don't really know.

Friend: But it's up to you how you use your profiles. I have mine purely for professional purposes.

Beatrice: Seriously? Only for that?

Friend: Of course. No children's photos, no holiday posts. Just professional networking.

---

lost in thought 생각에 잠긴 | **reason** 이유 | **invisible** 보이지 않는 | **purely** 순전히 | **professional purposes** 직업적인 목적

Dialogue 2

Beatrice: Oh sorry! I got lost in my thoughts for a moment there.
Friend: Is there something wrong?
Beatrice: I've just been reading an article about the Wiki pages, blogging, social networking ...
Friend: OK, and what about it?
Beatrice: I'm overwhelmed. There is just too much of everything.
Friend: But that's normal! Information overload is one of the major problems of the Internet era.
Beatrice: Really? I had no idea. So I'm not the only one drowning in tabs and bookmarks?
Friend: It sounds like you need a good bookmark manager, but that's not the real problem here.
Beatrice: It's not? But how else do I find the information I need?
Friend: You've got software for that. But what about the credibility of that information? Who's the source and what's at stake? Those are the real questions.

overwhelmed 압도된 ǀ **overload** 과부하 ǀ **drown** ~에 몰두하다; ~에 담그다 ǀ **credibility** 신뢰성 ǀ **what's at stake** 무엇이 중요한지

Dialogue 3

Beatrice: Look at this piece: Technology and medicine.
Friend: Sounds very interesting to me.
Beatrice: Well, it scares me.
Friend: Why?
Beatrice: Everything is happening so fast now.
Friend: And that worries you? Why on earth?
Beatrice: Not everything gets examined and tested properly.
Friend: There is always a chance for human error, true. But generally, we are better off with the advancements in medicine than without them.

Why on earth? 도대체 왜? ǀ **advancement** 진보

Vocabulary plus

account	계좌	infant mortality	유아 사망률
addictive	중독성의	intentionally	의도적으로
anxious	불안한	interfere	간섭하다
available	이용 가능한	keep the balance	균형을 유지하다
boundary	경계	leap	껑충 뛰다
careful	조심하는	lose it	미치다
catch up	따라잡다	means	수단
complaining	불평	milestone	중요한 사건
conscious consumer	의식있는 소비자	operative word	요점
contact lenses	콘택트렌즈	over the centuries	수세기에 걸쳐
countless	무수한	overreact	과잉 반응을 보이다
crutch	목발	pacemaker	심박 조율기
double-edged sword	양날의 검	policy	정책
easily accessible	쉽게 접근할 수 있는	proceed with caution	조심스럽게 진행하다
frankly speaking	솔직히 말해서	rely	의지하다
frightening	무서운	source of knowledge	지식의 출처
general anaesthetic	전신 마취	stem cell research	줄기세포 연구
get off one's high horse	잘난 체하는 태도를 버리다	surgery	수술
Give me a break.	그만 좀 해!	take advantage of	이용하다
head	향하다	Take it easy.	진정하세요.
health records	건강 기록	tick	체크 표시를 하다
impatience	성급함	tool	도구
in depth	심도 있게	wheelchair	휠체어
		X-ray	엑스레이

Cultural tips

Did you know that ...?

There are many parks and open spaces in London. Green space in central London consists of eight Royal Parks (including the most famous Hyde Park, Green Park, Kensington Gardens etc.), supplemented by a number of small garden squares scattered throughout the city centre.

Scene 12 (36) — Film dialogue and vocabulary

Read the dialogue between Vlad (V) and Sergey (S). Check the list of words and phrases below.

You must tell him we ... er ...

S: Botched up the killing?

V: Botched up the killing!

S: I don't give a shit! I've been tricked by him ... again! But he's always been like that – he says one thing, means something else, but in the end ... it's all about him!

V: But he is ... what he is. Not much can be done to make him different. You need to understand his ... er ... obligations.

S: Yeah? Is your family okay with your obligations?

V: No, they weren't ... No! My son was like you. Good student, strong brain. Big man like me, but didn't like fighting. He had a kind heart. Like you! ... wanted to be a doctor. Can you imagine? My son – a doctor? And my wife ... well ... She was ...

S: They were killed, weren't they?

V: Half a year ago. ... I found each of the men who came to my house that night. Did bad things to them, took my time ... But too many questions were ... asked! So my bosses sent me to the UK to ... cool down here.

S: What am I supposed to do now? Go back home? Pretend my dad didn't try to turn me into a killer?

level B1

Vocabulary	botch up	망치다	imagine	상상하다
	trick	속이다	send	보내다
	obligation	의무	cool down	식히다
	brain	두뇌	killer	살인자
	doctor	의사		

What should Vlad do?

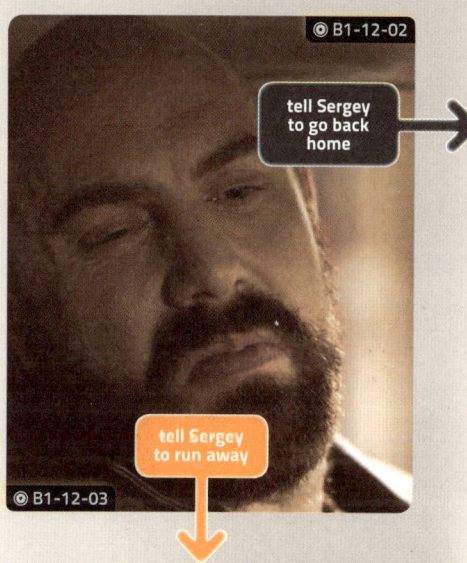

tell Sergey to go back home

tell Sergey to run away

V: Yes, go back to your father. He's getting old and he will need you to take over his business. You'll get used to this lifestyle – girls, heaps of money ... People pissing their pants when they see you!

S: Thank you, Vlad, but that's not me.

Vocabulary	lifestyle	생활
	heaps of	많은
	piss one's pants	오줌을 지리다

V: No, run as far from your father as you can. Pack your suitcase and go! I respect Gennady, but ... he's a devil. He will work on you until you are evil, like him!

S: He can't do that!

V: He can! He did it ... to me! Many years ago. And now look at Vlad – a crazy, mean bastard who should be put ... in prison until he dies.

pack	짐을 싸다	evil	악; 사악한
devil	악마		

Grammar explanations

과거 시제, 과거완료, 미래 시제의 수동태

수동태 = be동사 + 과거분사

➜ was/were + 과거분사

He **was given** the telephone number to Olive Green, a professional art thief.
그에게 미술품 전문 도둑인 Olive Green의 전화번호가 주어졌습니다.

➜ had been + 과거분사

When Robert opened the safety deposit box, the documents **had** already **been stolen**.
Robert가 귀중품 보관함을 열었을 때 문서는 이미 도난을 당한 상태였습니다.

➜ will be + 과거분사

The transaction between Olive and her boss **will be finalised** in a few hours.
Olive와 그녀의 보스 간의 거래는 몇 시간 후에 끝날 것입니다.

조동사가 들어 있는 문장의 수동태

긍정문인 경우: 조동사 + be동사 + 과거분사
부정문인 경우: 조동사 + not + be동사 + 과거분사

→ should (not) + be동사 + 과거분사

The report **should (not) be prepared** by our department. 보고서는 저희 부서에 의해 준비되어야 합니다.

→ ought (not) to + be동사 + 과거분사

Some works of art **ought (not) to be exhibited** in the open air.
몇몇 미술 작품은 야외에 전시되어야 합니다.

→ may (not) + be동사 + 과거분사

You **may (not) be asked** to answer all the questions in detail.
모든 질문에 자세히 답해 달라는 요청을 받을 수도 있습니다.

→ might (not) + be동사 + 과거분사

You **might (not) be given** additional information. 추가 정보가 주어질 수도 있습니다.

→ will (not) + be동사 + 과거분사

The exhibition **will (not) be held** in November. 전시회는 11월에 열릴 것입니다.

→ can (cannot) + be동사 + 과거분사

This error **can (cannot) be fixed** immediately. 이러한 실수는 당장 고쳐질 수 있습니다.

→ could (not) + be동사 + 과거분사

The door **could (not) be painted** a different colour immediately.
문은 즉시 다른 색으로 칠해질 수 있습니다.

→ must (not) + be동사 + 과거분사

The boss **must (not) be told** today. 보스는 오늘 이야기를 들어야 합니다.

Communication situations

Read the following dialogues between a Customer Service assistant and a dissatisfied customer.

> Good morning, welcome to Customer Service, how can I help you?

Dialogue 1

Client: Good morning, I bought a coffee machine last week and it doesn't work.

Assistant: OK. I'll have a look at it. In the meantime, please prepare the receipt or other proof of purchase.

Client: I have nothing with me but you should have this purchase in your database.

Assistant: Do you know how big the database is? Besides, a complaint is considered only if you provide proof of purchase.

Client: Could I speak to the manager, please?

Assistant: Of course. Just a moment, please.

---

receipt 영수증 | **proof of purchase** 구매 증빙 서류

Dialogue 2

Client: I'm calling in regard to the tablet I bought. I'm not satisfied with it.

Assistant: All right. What's wrong with the product?

Client: I think there is something wrong with the software. It's not compatible with most applications.

Assistant: I'm sorry to hear that. If you have all the data, meaning: purchase details and the catalogue number of your tablet, its series etc., we can solve the problem within 5 minutes.

Client: That's what I like. A really helpful customer service.

Assistant: Thank you. Hold on, please. I'll just ask an IT technician to get the details and take care of the case.

---

in regard to ~에 관해서 | **compatible** 호환이 되는 | **Hold on, please.** 끊지 말고 잠시만 기다려 주세요.

Dialogue 3

Client: I bought that in your online shop but there is a product failure so I'd like to exchange it.

Assistant: Exchanging the product is not a problem, as long as it has not been used, it's in its original packaging and you have got proof of purchase.

Client: OK. I've got it all.

Assistant: All right. Would you like the same model?

Client: Well, I'd like to have an upgraded version.

Assistant: OK, but you'll have to cover the difference in value.

Client: Actually, I think you should cover the difference as a compensation for me.

Assistant: I'm afraid that won't be possible.

Client: Really? That's just not fair!

Assistant: Why do you think it's unfair? A new model costs more. Why should we cover the difference?

Client: Never mind. I'll take the same model if that's the case.

Assistant: As you wish. Fill in this form, please.

---

failure 실패, 고장 | **exchange** 교환하다 | **upgraded** 개선된 | **value** 값 | **compensation** 보상 | **if that's the case** 그런 경우라면
fill in 작성하다 | **form** 양식

Vocabulary plus

accessories	부속품	hang up	전화를 끊다
acknowledge	인정하다	I'll be right back.	금방 다녀올게요.
appreciate	감사하다	item	항목
appropriate	적절한	loud	시끄러운
attach	붙이다	manufacturer	제조사
be aware of	~을 의식하다	manufacturing defect	제조상의 결함
be fed up with	~에 진저리가 나다	persist	고집하다
damaged	손상 입은	properly	제대로
fall short of expectations	기대에 못 미치다	refund	환불
faulty	결함 있는	repair	수리
flaw	결점	scratched	긁힌
from the beginning	처음부터	standard procedure	표준 절차
get clogged	막히다	take a photo	사진 찍다
gift-wrap	선물용으로 포장하다	tube	관, 통
give something a try	~을 한번 해보다	within the warranty service	보증 수리 기간 내
ground	갈은		

Cultural tips

Did you know that ...?

The **flag of the UK** is known as the "Union Flag" or, popularly, "Union Jack". It has the red cross of Saint George (patron saint of England), edged in white, on top of the Cross of Saint Patrick (patron saint of Ireland), on top of the Saltire of Saint Andrew (patron saint of Scotland).

The **flag of the U.S.** is known as the "Stars and Stripes", the "Star-Spangled Banner", or "Old Glory". It has 7 red stripes and 6 white stripes, which stand for the original 13 colonies. The flag also has a blue rectangle in the top left corner with one white star for every state.

Translation

Scene 1 (25)

Film dialogue and vocabulary p. 8~10

G: 15만 9천이야! (…) 잘 들어. 당신 아들이 도박에 빠져 산 지 최소한 반년은 됐어…

G: 주로 개들이지… "걔들"이라니 무슨 소리야? 개들 말이야! 아니! 개 경주 얘기가 아니야! 개싸움! 당신 아들이 한 번도 안 빠지고 투견 도박을 한 지 두 달이 넘었어!

W: 시간을 좀 주세요. 빌게요!

show no mercy

G: 자선사업 하는 줄 아나! 아들 빚을 갚아. 내일까지야. 그렇지 않으면 내 부하들이 아들을 찾아갈 거야. 내 말 알아들었나?

Y: 그런데요, 보스. 세르게이가 오늘 집에 오는 거 아니에요?

G: 내일이야. 나더러 자기 졸업식을 보러 옥스퍼드에 오라더군. 내가 보기엔 시간 낭비야! 하지만 나한테 계획이 있어! 일을 줄 거야! 쉬운 일이야! 초보자에겐 딱이지! 블라드와 짝을 지어줄 거야!

Y: 하지만… 블라드는… 망나니예요. 놈은…

G: 진짜 사나이지! 싸움꾼! 이 조직의 정통 멤버야. 난 내 아들이 그렇게 되길 바란다고! 그럼 내일… 이런 젠장!

S: 내 졸업식에 왜 안 오셨어요? 아침 내내 연락드렸는데요!

G: 세르게이, 사랑하는 내 아들!

show mercy

G: 알았어! 나도 아들이 하나 있는데 당신 아들처럼 아주 애물단지지! 2주 주지, 알겠나?

Y: 그런데요, 보스. 세르게이가 오늘 집에 오는 거 아니에요?

G: 내일이야. 나더러 자기 졸업식을 보러 옥스퍼드에 오라더군. 내가 보기엔 시간 낭비야! 하지만 나한테 계획이 있어! 일을 줄 거야! 쉬운 일이야! 초보자에겐 딱이지! 블라드와 짝을 지어줄 거야!

Y: 하지만 블라드는… 망나니예요. 놈은…

G: 진짜 사나이지! 싸움꾼! 이 조직의 정통 멤버야. 난 내 아들이 그렇게 되길 바란다고! 그럼 내일… 이런 젠장!

S: 내 졸업식에 왜 안 오셨어요? 아침 내내 연락드렸는데요!

G: 세르게이, 사랑하는 내 아들!

Communication situations p. 14~15

HR employee: 저희는 세계에서 5등 안에 드는 수문학 리서치 센터로, 직원들을 매우 까다롭게 뽑습니다. 세르게이, 당신은 물론 이곳에서의 짧은 인턴 경력이라도 당신의 경력에 큰 도움이 될 수 있다는 점을 알고 있을 것입니다. 이곳에서는 당신의 학력 사항이 중요하기 때문에 그에 관해서 저희에게 정확히 말씀을 해 주십시오.

Dialogue 1

Candidate: 알겠습니다. 유치원부터 시작해야 하나요?

HR employee: 그럴 필요는 없어요. 대신 중고등학교에 관한 이야기를 듣고 싶군요.

Candidate: 저는 홈스쿨링을 했습니다.

HR employee: 왜 홈스쿨링을 선택했나요?

Candidate: 질적인 면에서 개인 교습이 더 나은 해결책이었기 때문이었습니다.

HR employee: 어떤 이유로 공부를 계속했나요?

Candidate: 식수 시스템에 관한 논문으로 장학금을 받았습니다.

HR employee: 그리고 당신의 학력 사항 상 다음 단계는 대학이었고요, 그렇지 않나요?

Candidate: 네, 그렇습니다. 저는 옥스퍼드 대학에 지원했습니다.

HR employee: 금전적인 문제는 어떻게 했나요?

Candidate: 저는 장학금을 받았고 아프리카에서 1년을 보냈습니다.

HR employee: 그 후에는요?

Candidate: 온라인으로 지구과학 학사 학위 과정을 마쳤습니다.

HR employee: 그래요. 알겠어요. 대학원이나 박사 과정을 고려한 적이 있나요?

Candidate: 수문학 석사 학위를 받은 후에 박사 과정을 밟을 예정입니다.

HR employee: 시간을 내 줘서 고마웠어요. 일주일 내로 연락을 드릴게요.

Dialogue 2

HR employee: 중고등학교로 시작해 봅시다

Candidate: 저는 직업 학교에 다녔습니다.

HR employee: 어떤 교육을 받았나요?

Candidate: 저는 화훼 장식에 대해 배우기로 결심했습니다.

HR employee: 화훼 장식요? 왜 그 분야의 교육 과정을 선택했죠? 중첩되는 부분이 있다고 생각했나요?

Candidate: 계획은 없었고, 단지 새로운 것을 시도해 보고 싶었어요.

HR employee: 그리고 당신의 학력 사항 상 다음 단계는 대학이었고요, 그렇지 않나요?

Candidate: 아닙니다, 그렇지 않아요. 저는 1년 쉬기로 결심했습니다.

HR employee: 그 후에는요?

Candidate: 저는 백만장자가 되었습니다.

HR employee: 시간을 내 줘서 고마웠어요. 일주일 내로 연락을 드릴게요.

Dialogue 3

Candidate: 저는 런던 최고의 중고등학교를 졸업했습니다.

HR employee: 그리고 당신의 학력 사항 상 다음 단계는 대학이었고요, 그렇지 않나요?

Candidate: 네, 그렇습니다. 저는 옥스퍼드의 지구과학 학과에 입학했습니다.

HR employee: 금전적인 문제는 어떻게 했나요?

Candidate: 학자금 대출을 받아야 했습니다.

HR employee: 그래요. 알겠어요. 대학원이나 박사 과정을 고려한 적이 있나요?

Candidate: 먼저 수문학과 관련된 실무 경험을 쌓고 싶습니다.

Scene 2 (26)

Film dialogue and vocabulary   p. 18~20

G: 아직도 내 옛날 번호를 갖고 있나 보다.

G: 내가 번호를 얼마나 자주 바꿔야 하는지 알지? 2주 넘게 같은 번호를 쓰면 당장 경찰이 들이닥칠 거야.

S: 평범한 일을 하면 경찰이 괴롭히지 않을 거예요!

G: 내 일 덕분에 그놈의 옥스퍼드 학비도 내고 네가 타고 온 멋진 차도 사준 거야! 그러니까 나한테… 아들, 미안하다. 내가 잘못했어, 됐니? 나는 기뻐… 우리 가문에 생물학자가 있는 게 자랑스럽다.

S: 수문학자요!

G: 그래, 그래… 수문학자! 앉아… 너한테 줄 선물이 있어!

S: 이걸로 뭘 어쩌라고요?

G: 쏴!

S: 누굴 쏴요?

G: 아무나 쏘고 싶은 사람! 하지만 적당한 선은 지켜야 해, 알았지? 지긋지긋한 학교가 다 끝나서 너무 좋다. 사실, 너한테 일자리를 제안하마! 블라드를 도와줘. 러시아에서 온 새 직원인데, 사람을 찾는…

S: 아빠, 제발요. 말도 꺼내지 마세요!

G: 아니, 들어 봐, 네가 생각하는 그런 일이 아니라! 민감한 사업 문제야. 경찰이 끼어들면 안 돼. 블라드는 여기 처음 왔어. 영어도 못하고 지리도 몰라. 게다가, 이런 일을 할 만큼 머리가 좋지 못해.

S: 아빠, 난 못 해요!

`beg`

G: 아들, 부탁이야! 요즘엔 믿을 사람이 없어! 나도 늙었어. 도와달라고 부탁하는 거야. 생각해 봐, 여태 내가 널 키웠잖니!

S: 알았어요, 아빠. 이번 한 번만이에요! 그리고 뭐가 됐든… 폭력은 안 돼요.

G: 그건 걱정하지 마!

`make a threat`

G: 아들, 이 일을 안 할 거면 평범한 직업을 구해서 그동안 내가 너한테 준 돈 다 갚아. 그게 얼마나 될까? 최소한 수십만 파운드는 될 거야. 요즘 수문학자 수입이 얼마나 되지?

S: 알았어요, 아빠. 이번 한 번만이에요! 그리고 뭐가 됐든… 폭력은 안 돼요.

G: 그건 걱정하지 마!

Communication situations   p. 23~25

Student A: 이번 시험이 걱정돼. 가장 어려운 시험 중에 하나라고 하더군. 오랫동안 힘들게 배웠지만 시험 준비가 되어있는지는 잘 모르겠어.

Dialogue 1

Student B: 무슨 말인지 알아. 함께 한 번 더 복습하자.

Student A: 정말 좋은 생각이야. 그러면… 흠, 그래. 퀴즈 내기는 어때? 어떤 계통이나 기관을 짧게 설명하고 그 다음에 답을 하는 걸로.

Student B: 좋아. 나부터 시작할게.

Student A: 그래. 골격계로 시작할까? 내가 가장 좋아하는 부분이거든.

Student B: 물론이지. 두개골에서 유일하게 움직이는 뼈의 명칭은 무엇이지?

Student A: 쉽네! 턱뼈잖아! 내 차례야. 손에는 몇 개의 뼈가 있지?

Student B: 양손에?

Student A: 응, 3개나 그 이상을 갖고 있는 것이 아니라면. 대답해 봐!

Student B: 모두 합쳐 54개.

Student A: 분류할 수 있어?

Student B: 그래. 엄지에 2개에다가, 각 손가락에 3개가 있고, 손바닥에 5개, 그리고 손목에 8개가 있지.

Student A: 와, 굉장한걸! 정말 시험 준비가 잘 되어 있구나!

Dialogue 2

Student B: 무슨 말인지 전적으로 이해해. 함께 검토해 보는 것이 어떨까?

Student A: 정말 좋은 생각이야. 그러면… 흠, 그래. 퀴즈 내기는 어때? 어떤 계통이나 장기를 짧게 설명하고 그 다음에 답을 하는 걸로.

Student B: 그래, 안 될 것 없지. 해 볼까?

Student A: 응, 나는 준비됐어. 먼저 순환계부터 다루자.

Student B: 두 개의 주요 혈관계를 뭐라고 부르지?

Student A: 체정맥과 체동맥.

Student B: 정맥의 기능은 무엇이지?

Student A: 혈액을 심장으로 돌려 보내.

Student B: 잘 했어! 나는 항상 두 계통이 헷갈리거든!

Student A: 오 이런, 정말이야? 그렇다면 시험을 볼 때에는 정말로 주의해야 해!

Dialogue 3

Student B: 순환계 기관의 주요 기능은 무엇이지?

Student A: 음, 어떤 기관을 의미하느냐에 따라 답이 달라져.

Student B: 비강으로 시작하자.

Student A: 코에 대해 이야기하고 싶은 거니? 좋아. 공기가 허파에 들어가기 전에 공기를 준비해 주지.

Student B: 그래, 공기를 정화하고 따뜻하게 만들고 공기에 수분을 줘.

Student A: 그래, 맞아. 이제 다음 문제로 넘어가면…

Scene 3 (27)

Film dialogue and vocabulary　p. 28~29

S: 블라드, 팔꿈치 좀 치워주세요… 레버에서요.

S: 내가 가서 보고 올게요. 당신은 차에 있어요, 알았죠? 분명히 말해 두는데, 아무 버튼이나 만지면 안 돼요! 그냥 앉아서 아무것도 하지 말아요! 아뇨, 블라드! 차에 있어야 해요! 사람들 눈에 띄면 안 되잖아요! 자연스럽게 – 그게 우리 목표예요! 알았어요? 왜요? 원하는 게 뭐예요?

V: 내 총! 가져가! 작은 사람은 총이 있어야 해!

G: 선생님, 차 좀 치워주시죠! 저기에 주차하시면 안 됩니다!

V: 내 차 아냐!

G: 차에 앉아서 운전자와 얘기하는 걸 봤습니다. 운전자에게 전화해서 이동하라고 하십시오! 어서요! (…) 선생님, 거기 서세요! (…) 어쩔 수 없군요!

S: 정말 죄송합니다. 뭐가 문제죠?

Communication situations　p. 32~33

Police officer: 앉으세요. 당신의 진술을 들어야 하는데, 약간의 시간이 걸릴 수도 있습니다. 어떤 일이 있었는지 설명해 주시겠어요?

Dialogue 1

Victim: 제가 강도를 당하다니 아직도 몸이 떨리는군요.

Police officer: 이해합니다. 유쾌한 기분은 아니죠. 언제, 그리고 어디에서 강도를 당하셨나요?

Victim: 모든 일은 두 시간 전 저희 집 근처 거리에서 일어났어요.

Police officer: 그렇군요. 그런데 어디에서 사시나요?

Victim: Queen 가에 살고 있어요.

Police officer: 범인을 보셨나요?

Victim: 아니요, 모든 일이 너무 빨리 벌어졌어요.

Police officer: 그렇다면 조사는 끝났습니다. 강도를 찾을 수 있는 가능성은 전혀 없습니다.

Dialogue 2

Victim: 휴가 기간에 도둑이 들었어요.

Police officer: 왜 그렇게 생각하시죠?

Victim: 음, 저희가 도착했을 때 집이 크게 어질러져 있었기 때문에 저는 누군가가 침입을 했다고 확신해요.

Police officer: 이웃들은요? 무언가를 본 사람이 있었나요?

Victim: 아니요, 없는 것 같아요. 보았다면 누군가가 도둑질을 신고했을 거예요.

Police officer: 그럴 수도 있고 아닐 수도 있죠. 저희가 곧 이웃 사람들을 면담할 거예요. 이제 절도 행위에 대해 이야기하죠. 없어진 것이 있나요?

Victim: 네, 개인 소장품 중 두 점의 회화가 없어졌어요.

Police officer: 개인 소장품을 두고 계시지만 도난 경보 장치는 설치되어 있지 않군요?

Victim: 집 외부에 있는 도난 경보 장치가 절단되어 있었어요.

Police officer: 좋습니다. 도둑이 전문가였던 것으로 판명되는군요.

Dialogue 3

Victim: 저는 지난주 은행 강도 사건의 인질 중 한 명이었어요.

Police officer: 그래요, 알겠습니다. 물 한 잔 드세요. 많이 놀라신 것 같군요. 당신을 괴롭히는 무언가가, 혹은 누군가가 있나요? 정신 상담이 필요하신가요?

Victim: 네, 도움이 필요한 것 같아요. 잠을 잘 수가 없고, 그렇지 않으면 악몽을 꾸어요.

Police officer: 이해가 됩니다. 잠시 시간을 주시면 제가 정신과 의사 선생님께 연락을 드릴게요.

Scene 4 (28)

Film dialogue and vocabulary   p. 36~38

V: 내가 들어가서… 얘기할 거야! 얘기해서 해결책을… 찾을 거야! 돌아올게! 넌 입구를 지켜. 놈들이 나오면 네가 막아!

O: 항상 이해가 안 되는 게 남자들 사이에 폴로 셔츠가 인기 있다는 거예요. 왜 그런 걸 입고 싶어 할까요?

O: 그걸 입으면 꼭… 샌님 같아 보이는데 말이죠. 옷깃 세우는 건 또 어떻고요! 패션 테러예요! 그냥 티셔츠가 훨씬 더 잘 어울릴 것 같아요. 검은색, 흰색, 빨간색도요… 빨간색은… 입은 걸 내가 먼저 봐야겠지만요.

D: 올리브, 잠깐 나 좀 혼자 있게 해줄래요?

V: 폴로 셔츠! 끔찍한 발명품이지! 어떻게 생각해? 이런 걸 입으면 내가 영국인 같아 보일까? 자연스러워 보일까… 올리브?

D: 젠장 내 손!

V: 우린 다시 가게로 가! 네가 내 폴로 셔츠 계산해!

Communication situations p. 40~41

Wife: 호텔, 패키지 여행, 그리고 수영장은 지겨워. 올해는 다른 것을 해 보자. 아이들에게 야생 지역을 보여 주는 것은 어떨까?

Dialogue 1

Husband: 그래, 나도 같은 생각이야. 우리에게는 변화가 필요해.

Wife: 그러면, 아이디어라도 있어? 아마도 걷기 여행?

Husband: 물론 있지. 인터넷에서 맞춤형 여행에 대해 알아보자.

Wife: 그 말이 아니야. "패키지" 여행과 "맞춤형" 여행 간에는 아무런 차이가 없어. 둘 다 값만 비싸고 뻔한 것들이지.

Husband: 그러면, 사이클링 투어에 대해서는 어떻게 생각해?

Wife: 괜찮아. 생각해 둔 것이라도 있어?

Husband: 사실, 그래. '해안 자전거 전용 도로'야.

Wife: 흥미롭게 들리는군. 인터넷으로 자세한 내용을 확인해 보자.

Husband: 이곳 컴브리아의 서쪽 해안가로부터 시작하는 것을 추천하는군.

Wife: 잘 됐네. 나는 컴브리아에 가 본 적이 없어.

Husband: 좋아. 그러면 레이크 디스트릭트를 가로질러서 북동쪽 해안인 선더랜드에서 끝을 낼 수 있을 거야.

Wife: 계획이 마음에 들어. 정말로 다 살펴볼 수 있도록 서두르지 말고 천천히 가자. 굉장히 멋질 것 같아.

Dialogue 2

Husband: 그렇게 말해 주니 기쁘군. 좋은 생각이야.

Wife: 영국 내에 있는 시골길을 알아보는 것은 어때? '로빈 후드 길'에 대해 들은 적이 있어. 어떻게 생각해?

Husband: 아이들이 좋아할 것 같아.

Wife: 기다려 봐, 웹사이트를 찾아볼게. 좋아, 여기를 한 번 봐.

Husband: 168km에 이르는군. 우리에게 너무 길지 않을까?

Wife: 맞아. 초보자들에게는 꽤 먼 거리지.

Husband: 음, 전체 거리 중 일부만 걸을 수도 있어.

Wife: 그렇다면 나는 가장 흥미진진한 부분을 걷겠어. 셔우드에서 캠핑을 할 수 있을 것이라고 생각해?

Husband: 아니… 하지만 '로빈 후드 축제'가 열릴 때 갈 수 있을 거야.

Wife: 그것 좋은 생각이네! 한 번 볼게… 8월에 열려. 휴가를 보내기에 완벽한 시기야!

Dialogue 3

Husband: '1066 컨트리 걷기'는 어때?

Wife: 그에 대해서는 들어본 적이 없어. 더 말해 봐.

Husband: 그림과 같이 아름다운 오래된 마을을 시작으로 영국의 동남부를 가로질러 가는 거야.

Wife: "펜븐지" 맞지? 마치 '나니아'에서 온 아이들처럼?

Husband: 그래. 그리고 그곳 전원 지역은 15세기 이후로 크게 변하지 않았어. 멋질 것 같아.

Wife: 하지만, 남부를 방문하는 대신 해안과 바다를 포기하는 것은 안타까운 일 같은데.

Husband: 둘 다 선택할 수는 없잖아.

Scene 5 (29)

Film dialogue and vocabulary   p. 44~45

S: 고삐 풀린 망아지예요, 아빠! 정말이에요! 정신 나간 미치광이요! 대체 어디에서 데려온 거예요?

G: 잘 들어! 내가 블라드를 안 지는 25년 됐어. 그거 아니? 내 목숨도 한 번 구해줬어. 1988년 러시아에서 만났어. 페레스트로이카 때였지… 똑똑한 인간들은 쉽게 부자가 될 수 있었어. 내가 그랬지. 당시 블라드는 소년이었고, 18살인데, 덩치는 이미 거구였어. 하지만… 몹시 가난했어. 버려진 음식을 먹곤 했지. 화려한 호텔 뒷골목의 쓰레기통을 뒤져서… 세르게이, 넌 모를 거야. 가난이 사람을 어떻게 만드는지!… 암튼, 그래서 내가 거둬줬지. 블라드가… 빚도 받아주고, 심부름도 하고… 내 보디가드 노릇도 해줬어. 어느 날, 몇 명의 남자들과 거래를 마무리하는 날이었지. 친구인 줄 알았는데, 함정이었어. 같이 술 마시고 떠들다가 갑자기 놈들이 손에 칼을 들고 설치더니 순식간에 난 배를 찔리고 말았지. 블라드가 어떻게 했는지 아니? 다섯 명이었어! 맨손으로! 그러고는 날 병원에 데려갔어. 나중에 들었는데 모스크바 시내를 걸어왔다더군. 피범벅이 된 채… 악마처럼! 요즘은… 내가 블라드한테 빚이 많아. 게다가… 최근에… 개인적으로 슬픈 일을 겪었어. 영국에 온 건 선택의 여지가 없었기 때문이야. 블라드는 여길 싫어해. 아마… 우울할 거야. 그러니까 네가 영어도 가르쳐주고, 구경도 시켜주고… 일을 마무리하게 도와줘! 블라드에겐 일이 필요해! 아무런 할 일도 없으면 호텔 방에 앉아서 벽만 보고 있을 거야. 불쌍하지! 난 블라드가 다시 행복해지길 바래!

S: 알았어요. 제가 운전사 노릇 할게요! 하지만 이건 약속해요. 누굴 죽이는 건 못 도와줘요!

G: 당연하지! 블라드가 겁만 좀 주고 훔쳐간 물건을 돌려받을 거야. 그래, 약간 손봐줄 수는 있어! 하지만 약속하마, 아무도 안 죽일 거야!

S: 가죠, 블라드! 그 사람들 잡으러 가요!

Communication situations   p. 48~49

Gennady: 블라드, 영국으로 와 줘서 기쁘군. 드디어 이곳에서 네가 필요해 졌어. 하지만 나를 위한 일을 하기에 앞서 먼저 법적인 문제들을 처리해야 해. 영국 시스템에서 네가 보이고 인식될 수 있도록 해야 하지. 그리고 난 후에 너를 위한 일을 마련해 줄 수 있어.

Dialogue 1

Vlad: 저를 위한 일이라고요? 저는 당신을 위해 일하기로 되어 있지 않나요?

Gennady: 결과적으로는 그렇지. 하지만 먼저 합법적인 외국인 노동자로서, 모든 영국 데이터베이스에서 네가 보일 수 있도록 해야 해. 어떻게 하고 싶은가?

Vlad: 돈벌이가 된다면 무엇이든 할 수 있어요.

Gennady: 흠, 그래. 여기에서는 그곳에 월급이 있고 임금이 있다는 것을 기억하도록 해.

Vlad: 이곳에서는 초과 근무 수당을 받나요?

Gennady: 일반적으로는 그렇지.

Vlad: "일반적"이라고요? 받는다는 건가요, 받지 않는다는 건가요?

Gennady: 나를 위해 일을 할 때에는 초과 근무가 없어. 성과급이기 때문에 초과 근무 수당은 지급되지 않지. 하지만 일반적인 회사에서는, 맞아, 보통 초과 근무 수당이 지급되지.

Dialogue 2

Vlad: 좋아요, 보스. 첫 번째 단계가 무엇이죠?

Gennady: NINO를 가지고 있나?

Vlad: 없는 것 같은데요. 그게 뭐죠?

Gennady: 국민 보험 번호야. 영국 시스템에서 네가 인식될 수 있도록 만들어 주는 공식 문서지. 그에 대해서는 내가 알아보도록 할게. 그럼, 취업 허가증은?

Vlad: 음, 제가 국민 보험 번호를 가지고 있지 않다면 취업 허가증도 마찬가지로 없는 거겠죠, 그렇죠?

Gennady: 그래, 좋은 지적이군. 네 생각이 놀랄 정도로 빠르다는 점은 인정해야겠어.

Dialogue 3

Vlad: 먼저 일을 찾아보죠. 서류 작업은 어쨌든 이틀이면 끝날 테니까요.

Gennady: 그래, 맞는 말 같군. 신문을 하나 가져 올게.

Vlad: 러시아에서는 보통 인터넷에서 일자리를 찾아요. 여기에서도 똑같이 하지 않나요?

Gennady: 영국 사람들도 그렇게 할 수는 있겠지만, 나는 전통주의자야. 취업 섹션이 잘 되어 있는 신문이 필요해.

Vlad: 하지만 왜 신문이 필요한 건데요? 모든 것은 인터넷에 있어요.

Gennady: 신문이 먼저이고 인터넷은 나중이야. 자, 여기에 무엇이 있지?

Vlad: 이것을 보면: "저희는 회사차, 컴퓨터, 그리고 개인 사무실을 제공해 드립니다"라고 되어 있네요.

Gennady: 휴일 근무 수당이나 병가 수당에 대한 말도 하고 있나?

Vlad: 아니요, 그렇지 않아요.

Gennady: 그러면 그냥 놔 둬. 사회 보장 제도가 적용되지 않으면 고려해볼 가치가 없어.

Scene 6 (30)

Film dialogue and vocabulary   p. 52~53

D: 좋은데요, 올리브. 여기 자주 와요?

O: 런던에 올 때마다요… 질문도 없고 시간당 요금도 아주 저렴하거든요!

O: 자, 손 좀 보여줘요!

D: 부러진 것 같아요! 부러진 게 확실해요!

O: 아뇨! 기껏해야 탈골이에요! 자기, 우리 관계에 관해 얘기 좀 해!

D: 정말요?

O: 그래, 자기!

O: 가게에서 만난 덩치 큰 남자요… 억양을 보면 러시아인 같아요. 청부살인업자가 틀림없어요. 우릴 다시 보는 순간 죽일 게 분명해요.

D: 경찰에 신고해야 하지 않을까요? 우리끼리는 감당이 안 돼요!

O: 데이비드, 영국 경찰에 대한 신뢰가… 감동적이네요. 하지만 경찰이 우릴 보호해주진 못해요. 오늘 밤에 일을 끝내고 같이 사라지면 돼요!

D: 같이 사라져요? 이 모든 상황을 뒤로하고요? 왜 내 방식대로 하면 안 되는데요?

argue

O: 난 도둑이에요! 경찰에 신고 안 해요. 도망 다닌다고요!

D: 난 경찰관이에요. 죄를 지은 사람들이 벌을 받게 하죠! 생각 좀 해봐야겠어요.

give up

O: 좋아요! 그게 최선이라고 생각한다면… 경찰에 전화해요.

D: 생각 좀 해봐야겠어요.

Communication situations p 56~58

Friend: 베아트리스? 너니? 나 기억해? 몇 년 전에 같은 학교를 다녔잖아.

Dialogue 1

Beatrice: 오, 깜짝이야! 내 첫 번째 남자 친구를 어떻게 잊겠어? 어떻게 지내니?

Friend: 잘 지내, 고마워! 내 걱정은 마. 너를 봐! 많이 변했는걸!

Beatrice: 시간이 꽤 지났어. 사람들은 변해, 그렇지?

Friend: 물론. 그러면 어떻게 살고 있어? 결혼은 했니, 아니면 혼자야?

Beatrice: 실은, 혼자야.

Friend: 나도 그래. 어찌됐든 우리가 헤어지지 말았어야 했는데.

Beatrice: 정말로 열정적인 시간을 함께 보냈지, 그건 사실이야.

Friend: 오 그래, 그랬어. 그런데 우리가 왜 헤어졌지?

Beatrice: 솔직하게 말해? 이제는 기억나지가 않아.

Friend: 나도 마찬가지야. 심각한 건 아니었을 거야. 그렇다면 술이나 한 잔 할까?

Beatrice: 아니. 같은 강물에 두 번 발을 담글 수는 없어.

Friend: 오, 제발, 그냥 한 잔 하자는 거야. 옛날을 생각해서.

Dialogue 2

Beatrice: 그래, 기억 나.

Friend: 어… 그러면, 어떻게 지내니? 네가 굉장히 멋져 보인다고 말해야겠는걸!

Beatrice: 고마워. 미안하지만, 너하고 이야기하고 싶지는 않아.

Friend: 그렇군. 이유를 물어봐도 될까?

Beatrice: 학창 시절 너에 대한 기억이 좋지가 않아서야.

Friend: 오, 그래. 그때는 내가 너한테 그다지 다정하지 못했지. 커피 한 잔 하면서 그 때의 일을 정리할 수도 있지 않을까?

Beatrice: 아니, 나는 그렇게 생각하지 않아.

Friend: 알겠어. 이해해. 음, 다시 만나서 기뻤어. 잘 지내! 안녕!

Dialogue 3

Beatrice: 오, 깜짝이야! 내 첫 번째 남자 친구를 어떻게 잊겠어? 어떻게 지내니?

Friend: 잘 지내, 고마워! 내 걱정은 마. 너를 봐! 많이 변했는걸!

Beatrice: 음, 그래. 알겠지만 내 일 때문이야.

Friend: 네가 전임 환경운동가가 되고 싶어했다는 점이 기억 나. 하지만 환경운동가는 아닌 것 같은데, 내 말 맞니?

Beatrice: 그럼, 그건 어렸을 때의 꿈이었지. 나는 군인이야.

Friend: 다시 말해 줄래? 농담하는 거지?

Beatrice: 음, 지금 군복을 입고 있지는 않지만, 맞아, 나는 군인이야.

Friend: 어떻게 그렇게 됐니?

Beatrice: 음, 나는 항상 반대파였잖아, 기억해?

Friend: 그래! 하지만 체제에 대해 반대했지, 체제를 찬성하는 쪽은 아니었잖아!

Beatrice: 우리가 헤어지고서 상황이 바뀌었어.

Friend: 나 때문에 군인이 되었다고 말하지는 마!

Beatrice: 아니야. 부분적으로는 내가 받은 장학금 때문이었어.

Friend: 오, 장학금은 좋은 아이디어가 아니라고 알고 있었는데. 농담이야! 한 잔 하면서 그에 관한 이야기를 모두 해 줄 수 있니? 내가 살 게. 물론 네가 괜찮다면 말이야.

Scene 7 (31)

Film dialogue and vocabulary p. 60~61

V: 넌 여기 있어!

S: 명심해요! 살인은 안 돼요! 우리 아버지가 시킨 대로 해요!

V: 뭐?

S: 뭐가 뭐예요? 내가 이 일을 맡을 때, 아버지와 폭력에 관해 의논했어요. 아버지가 당신한테 설명해줬다고 했어요. 우리는… 당신은 그들을 손만 약간 봐주고 도둑맞은 걸 되찾기만 하는 거예요, 맞죠?

V: 그렇게 말했다고?

S: 아버지가 약속했어요!

V: 좋아, 어디 보자고! 넌… 내 뒤를 봐 줘! 무슨 일이 생기면… 그 총을 써!

D: 이렇게 말하는 거야… 올리브, 이제 결정을 내려야… 이런, 젠장!

`negotiate`

D: 해치지 않을 겁니다. 이거 보이죠? 난 경찰입니다! 그 총 버려요!

S: 이 총은… 난 쓸 줄도 몰라… (…) 블라드! 도와줘요!

`attack`

S: 안 돼요, 제발!

Communication situations   p. 64~65

Psychologist: 안녕하세요 올리브, 들어 오세요. 오늘은 평소보다 일찍 오셨군요. 눈이 빨갛고 부어 보이네요. 기쁨의 눈물이었나요, 아니면 슬픔의 눈물이었나요? 무슨 일이 있었죠, 올리브?

`Dialogue 1`

Olive: 네, 어제부터 많이 울었어요. 절망적이에요.

Psychologist: 자신에게 너무 혹독하게 굴지 말아요. 자, 앉으세요. 여기 물을 드릴게요. 자, 어떤 일이 있었나요?

Olive: 저는 어제 어떤 사람으로부터 비난을 받았는데, 그의 의견은 제게 많은 것을 의미해요.

Psychologist: 그러면 당신은 어떻게 반응했나요?

Olive: 저는 즉시 화를 냈어요. 실은, 격노를 했죠.

Psychologist: 무엇이 격노하도록 만들었나요?

Olive: 사장님께서 제가 본인을 실망시켰다고 말씀하셨어요.

Psychologist: 그런 말을 들었을 때 기분이 어땠나요?

Olive: 마치 숙제를 못한 여학생처럼 느껴졌어요.

Psychologist: 사장님께서 당신의 선생님이 되었군요. 그리고 당신은 스스로에 대한 믿음을 잃었고요. 그런 상황이 다시 일어나도록 하면 안 돼요.

`Dialogue 2`

Olive: 네, 울었지만 기뻐서 울었어요!

Psychologist: 좋은 소식이군요. 어떤 일이 있었나요?

Olive: 어제 드디어 '모나리자'를 훔쳤어요!

Psychologist: 뭐라고요? 아무 말도 하지 말아요! 경찰이 당신을 찾는 경우 경찰에게 질문을 받고 싶지는 않으니까요!

Olive: 오, 그러지 마세요. 저는 정말 흥분되어 있다고요!

Psychologist: 분명 그러실 테지만, 조심스럽게 말하면, 저는 그에 대해 복잡한 감정이 드네요.

Olive: 분위기 망치지 마세요. 저는 너무 기뻐요.

Psychologist: 네. 그리고 저는 겁나서 꼼작하지 못하겠어요.

Dialogue 3

Olive: 제 동료 때문이에요. 그가 저를 미치게 만들어요.

Psychologist: 좋아요. 당신이 화가 난 이유는 묻지 않을게요. 생산적이 될 수 있도록 그에 대한 대처 방법에 집중해 보죠.

Olive: 아니요, 그에 대해서는 이미 이야기를 했어요.

Psychologist: 그렇기는 하지만 제가 기대하는 만큼 당신이 안정적으로는 보이지 않아서요.

Olive: 제 안에 증오심이 너무 커요.

Psychologist: 그래요, 알겠어요. 그렇다면 결국 당신에 관한 이야기로 끝이 나겠군요. 좋습니다.

Scene 8 (32)

Film dialogue and vocabulary p. 68~69

V: 머리 다 감을 때까지 기다렸어.

V: 머리카락 관리가 내 아내한테도 중요했으니까 아내는 너보다 덩치가 컸어… 키도 크고, 아름답고, 자존심 강한 여자였지. 황소처럼 힘이 셌어! 가끔 나한테 화를 내면 내가 겁이 났지. 여기에 살이 더 많았어. 훨씬 많았어. 하지만 눈은… 너랑 똑같았어! (…) 내가… 총알을 빼놨어. 그러니까 총질은 안 돼. 자, 서류를 내놓으시지.

D: 개!

S: 내가 먼저 얘기해 볼게요!

S: 정신병자에 못 말리는 살인 기계예요! 싸우기 시작하면 우린 다 죽을 거예요!

D: 한 대 더 맞기 전에 닥쳐!

V: 봤지, 세르게이? 내가 약간… 손 봐줬어! 하지만 아주 멀쩡해.

Communication situations p. 72~74

Olive: 자기 안녕, 무슨 일이에요? 리스트에 있는 것을 모두 찾았나요?

Dialogue 1

David: 아니요, 하지만 크리스마스 쇼핑은 오늘이 마지막이에요!

Olive: 그래, 알겠어요. 크리스마스 장식이 있는 코너를 찾아서 리스트에 있는 것들을 하나씩 구해 봐요.

David: 좋아요. 조명용품. 올해 우리가 찾고 있는 것이 정확히 뭐죠?

Olive: 거실에 쓰일 장식 조명이에요.

David: 이것이 예쁘군요. 8개의 꼭지로 되어 있고 하얀색이고 철로 된 별이에요. 물론 LED 등도 들어 있어요.

Olive: 오, 크리스마스트리에 걸면 멋있게 보이겠네요. 사세요.

Dialogue 2

David: 아뇨. 그것이 바로 제가 전화한 이유에요. 저는 지금 소품 파는 곳에 있어요.

Olive: 그래, 알겠어요. 크리스마스 장식이 있는 코너를 찾아서 리스트에 있는 것들을 하나씩 구해 봐요.

David: 그래요. 장식용품 코너. 오, 여기에 정말로 멋진 소품들이 몇 개 있어요.

Olive: 우리가 빨간색 제품과 금색 제품을 찾고 있다는 걸 기억해요. 뭐가 보이나요?

David: 금? 저는 금처럼 예의가 바르죠. ('as good as gold 예의가 바른)

Olive: 알아요, 자기. 하지만 크리스마스트리에 자기를 걸 수는 없잖아요, 그렇죠?

David: 그래요. 나무로 된 것, 종이로 된 것, 아니면 플라스틱으로 된 것을 찾아 볼까요?

Olive: 재료는 그다지 중요하지 않아요. 모양에만 집중해요.

David: 작고, 나무로 만들어졌고, 빨갛고 하얀 눈송이들이 여기에 있어요. 매우 예쁜데. 관심이 있나요?

Olive: 네. 빨간색이고 금색인 것을 찾기만 하면 돼요, 그러면 되죠.

Dialogue 3

David: 농담하는 거죠! 저는 장난감 매장에 있어요. 여기에 있는 모든 것들은 다 똑같이 생겼고요.

Olive: 그건 불가능해요. 숨을 크게 쉬고 진싸로 주먹을 눌러봐요.

David: 모든 것이 연한 분홍색이거나 연한 파란색이에요. 그리고 알록달록한 색의 사탕을 보니 이빨이 썩을 것 같아요.

Olive: 음, 아이들을 위한 매장이잖아요. 무엇을 기대하나요?

David: 정말로 혼란스럽군요. 지금 어디로 가야 할지 모르겠어요.

Olive: 여자 아이를 위한 인형을 살 것이니까 이제 핑크색 코너로 가서 뭐가 보이는지 말을 해 주세요.

David: 네, 왔어요. 오 세상에, 한 곳에 이렇게 많은 인형이 건 결코 본 적이 없어요…

Olive: 자기야 진정해요, 너무 흥분하지 말고요. 하나만 골라서 나한테 설명해 주세요.

David: 촉감은 좋아요. 약간 보송보송하고 갈색 곱슬머리를 지니고 있군요.

Olive: '테디 베어'는 아닌 것이 확실하죠?

David: 저를 믿어요, 자기. 제가 어렸을 때 자동차만 갖고 논 것은 아니거든요.

Olive: 좋아요. 당신 마음에 들면 담아요.

David: 좋아요. 코너 한 개는 끝냈군요.

Olive: 그래요? 곧 다 끝날 거예요.

Scene 9 (33)

Film dialogue and vocabulary   p. 76~77

V: 나한테 말하기가 싫은가 봐… 강한 여자지만… 멍청해.
D: 총 버려! 아니면 이 사람을 죽이겠어!
V: 그럴 거야? 정말? 아니! 넌 겁먹었어! 정신이 하나도 없지!
D: 내 정신은 멀쩡해!
V: 이봐! 우린 그 서류가 필요해… 하지만 너희들까지 죽일 필요는 없어. 세르게이, 말해 줘! 저들을 죽일 필요는 없지, 안 그래? 훔쳐간 서류나 넘겨! 그럼 아무 문제 없어! 다들 만족하는 거지! 응?
O: 데이비드, 주면 안 돼요!

don't listen to Olive

O: 왜 그런 거예요? 왜?
V: 왜긴! 널 지키려는 거지! 멍청하긴! 미안!

listen to Olive

D: 아니, 거짓말이잖아!
V: 맞아! 좋아! 본론으로… 들어가지!
S: 뭐 하는 거예요, 블라드?
V: 너희 아버지가 시킨 거야! 데이비드, 마지막 기회야!
D: 좋아, 다 죽어보자고! 이 친구로 시작하지! 영 맘에 안 들어!
S: 안 돼요! 그러지 말아요, 제발요!
V: 그만! 쏘지 마! 부탁이야! 너희 아버지한테 이럴 순 없어, 세르게이! 하나밖에 없는 자식이잖아!

Communication situations   p. 80~81

Mother: 안녕, 그냥 인사하고, 시험 전날 어떻게 지내고 있는지 확인하려고 들렸단다. 책상 앞에 앉아 있지 않은 걸 보니 분명 잘 되고 있는 것 같구나.

Dialogue 1

Daughter: 보세요. 침대에 누워있는 것이 제가 긴장을 하지 않았다든가 시험 준비가 되어 있지 않다든가를 의미하는 것은 아니에요.
Mother: 그와 정반대지. 네가 잘 준비되어 있다는 것을 증명해 주는걸.
Daughter: 맞아요. 마침내 머리가 좋으신 분을 만났군요.
Mother: 멋지구나! 그리고 네가 무언가를 읽고 있다는 것도 알 수 있어.
Daughter: 네. 여자들 소설책이에요.

Mother: 여자들 소설? 부끄러운 줄 알거라.

Daughter: 왜요? 거기에는 잠재력이 있다고 생각해요.

Mother: 농담하는 거지, 그렇지 않니?

Daughter: 아니에요, 그렇지 않아요. 들어 보세요. 옛날 옛적에…

Mother: 그만하렴. 나는 결말을 알고 있단다. 그리고 그 후 그들은 행복하게 살았다…

Dialogue 2

Daughter: 네, 저는 괜찮아요. 준비 잘 하고 있어요. 지금은 쉬는 시간이에요.

Mother: 무엇을 읽고 있는지 보자. 흠. "올해 있었던 가장 재미있는 이야기 10선"이구나. 네가 지금 읽고 있는 이야기에 대해 말해 보렴.

Daughter: 죽은 캥거루에 관한 이야기예요.

Mother: 흥미롭게 들리는구나. 그에 대해 이야기해 줘.

Daughter: 음, 한 선원이 '아메리카 컵 요트 대회' 중 호주 해안가에 정박했어요.

Mother: 그리고…?

Daughter: 어느 날 그가 드라이브를 하러 갔어요. 무언가와 충돌했다고 느낀 순간에는 빠르게 차를 몰고 있었죠.

Mother: 그것이 캥거루였구나.

Daughter: 네. 분명 캥거루가 쓰러졌어요.

Mother: 오 이런! 불쌍한 것! 그 다음에 어떤 일이 일어났니?

Daughter: 캥거루가 잠시 후 깨어났을 때, 캥거루는 선원의 재킷을 입고 있었어요.

Mother: 캥거루가 그것을 좋아했니?

Daughter: 그걸 어떻게 알 수 있겠어요?

Mother: 그러면 요점이 뭐니?

Daughter: 모두 의미 없는 일로 끝이 났죠.

Mother: 아하. 그 점이 너를 웃게 만드는 거니?

Scene 10 (34)

Film dialogue and vocabulary p. 84

O: 당신 친구는 우리가 데려갈 거야! 그러니까 쫓아올 생각 마!

V: 두고 봐! 금방 쫓아갈 테니까!

D: 뭐죠?

O: 문이 부서진 거죠.

S: 블라드가 금방 쫓아온다고 했지만… 내가 설득해 볼게요. 꼭 피를 볼 필요는 없잖아요!

O: 데이비드! 드라이브나 가시지!

S: 제발요! 당신을 어떻게 찾았는지 말해줄게요!

O: 어떻게 찾았지?

S: 당신이 훔친 서류의 주인이 저 사람한테 준 폰을 추적했어요. 아버지한테 당신들을 찾아서 서류를 회수하고 죽이라고 한 것 같아요!

Communication situations   p. 88~89

Olive: … 그리고 나서 저는 휴대 전화를 끄고, 뜨거운 물로 샤워를 하고, 최대한 오래 잠을 잘 거예요!

Dialogue 1

David: 기다려요! 방송 들었나요?

Olive: 저는 모르겠어요. 당신 프랑스어 실력이 저보다 낫잖아요. 뭐라고 하던가요?

David: 비행기가 연착된 것 같아요.

Olive: 그럼 이제 어떻게 해야 하죠?

David: 이제 얼마나 연착될지 알아봐야 해요.

Olive: 몇 시간만 연착되고 하루 연착은 아니기를 바라보죠.

David: 하루 이상 연착되는 경우에는 항공사가 숙박을 제공해 줄 거예요.

Olive: 됐거든요! 저는 휴가가 빨리 시작되었으면 좋겠어요! 너무 오랫동안 기다렸는데 이제 이런 일이…

Dialogue 2

David: 잠시만요. 변경 사항이 있는 것 같아요.

Olive: 이런, 미안해요! 다시 한 번 말해 줄 수 없나요?

David: 잠깐 기다려 봐요. 안내 데스크로 가서 자세한 걸 물어볼게요.

(…)

Olive: 여자분이 뭐라고 말하던가요?

David: 짙은 안개 때문에 오늘 비행을 하지 못할 거래요.

Olive: 그렇군요. 여기에 발이 묶여 있는 건 우리뿐이 아닐 것이라고 확신해요. 환승에 대해서도 물어보았나요?

David: 아니요, 그러지 않았어요. 다시 가서 물어보죠. 다른 궁금한 점은요?

Olive: 수화물에 대해 물어봐 주세요. 수화물도 기다려야 하나요, 그렇지 않은가요?

David: 당신이 비행을 자주 하니 도움이 되는군요.

Olive: 그리고 당신은 프랑스어를 하잖아요! 천생연분이죠, 그렇지 않나요? 이제, 가서 물어보면 이 다음에 우리가 무엇을 해야 할지 정할 수 있을 거예요.

Dialogue 3

David: 쉿! 우리 비행기에 대해 무엇인가 말하지 않았나요?
Olive: 저는 모르겠어요, 당신 프랑스어 실력이 저보다 낫잖아요. 뭐라고 하던가요?
David: 우리가 게이트로 가야 할 것 같아요.
Olive: 게이트로요? 하지만 아직 체크인도 하지 않았는걸요!
David: 온라인으로 체크인을 했어요. 기억나지 않나요?
Olive: 오, 맞아요! 다행이네요! 그러면 게이트에 대해서는 어떤 내용이었나요?
David: 게이트가 열려서 탑승이 시작되었다고 말했어요.
Olive: 벌써요? 꽤 빠르군요. 먼저 면세점에 가고 싶었는데!

Scene 11 (35)

Film dialogue and vocabulary   p. 92~93

O: 머리 밑에서 일한다는 건 언제 얘기하려고 했어요?
D: 머리 밑에서 일하는 게 아니에요!
D: 그래요. 그건 맞지만, 머리가 날 협박한 거예요! 말하려고 했는데… 그 러시아인이 나타나는 바람에…
O: 협박요? 그래서 날 찾으려고 한 거예요?
D: 아뇨! 걱정돼서 찾으려고 한 거예요! 러시아 깡패도 아는 걸 당신은 왜 몰라요!
O: 오늘 저녁에 서류를 의뢰인에게 전달할 거예요. 현재로서는 그게 제일 중요해요. 당신이 있으면 내가 편해질 줄 알았는데, 그런데 아니에요! 방해만 되고 약점으로 작용하고 있어요… 이대로는 안 돼요! 오늘 밤에 거래를 성사시켜야 해요!
D: 그래요? 받을 돈 때문에요?
O: 아뇨! 당신만 협박당하는 거 아니에요. 나도 내가 아끼는 사람들을 지켜야 해요. 당신도 포함해서요!
D: 내 예전 삶을 포기하려고 했었어요. 하지만 우리 행동으로 너무 많은 사람이 다치게 돼요. 머리를 설득해 볼게요. 안 되면 그 서류가 뭐든… 언론에 알릴게요.

D: 지금은 내가 믿겠지만 언젠가 기회를 한 번 더 준다면…

Communication situations   p. 96~97

Friend: 안녕! 이봐, 베아트리스! 내 말 들려? 왜 그처럼 허공을 쳐다보고 있니?

Dialogue 1

Beatrice: 오 미안. 생각에 잠겨 있었어.

Friend: 그런 것 같구나. 무슨 이유로?

Beatrice: 먼저 내가 하나 물어볼게. 소셜 미디어를 사용하니?

Friend: 음, 물론 나는 온라인 상에 있어. 모두가 그렇잖아.

Beatrice: 음, 그것이 문제야. 나는 없거든.

Friend: 그렇다면, 몸을 숨기고 싶지 않는 이상, 시작해 봐.

Beatrice: 내 생활을 내가 실제로 모르는 "친구들"이라는 사람들과 공유하고 싶지는 않아.

Friend: 하지만 그건 네 프로필을 어떻게 사용하는지에 달렸어. 나는 순전히 직업적인 목적 때문에 가지고 있는걸.

Beatrice: 정말이야? 그것 때문에만?

Friend: 물론. 아이들 사진도 없고, 휴일 사진도 없어. 직업적인 네트워크일 뿐이지.

Dialogue 2

Beatrice: 오 미안! 잠시 생각 좀 하느라 정신이 없었네.

Friend: 잘못된 일이라도 있어?

Beatrice: 위키 페이지, 블로그, 소셜 네트워킹에 관한 기사를 읽고 있는 중이었는데…

Friend: 그래, 그런데 그게 어째서?

Beatrice: 감당이 안 돼. 모든 것들이 너무 많이 있잖아.

Friend: 하지만 그것이 정상인걸! 과도한 정보는 인터넷 시대의 주요 문제 중 하나라고.

Beatrice: 정말? 내가 몰랐네. 그러면 탭과 북마크에 허우적대고 있는 건 나 혼자가 아닌가?

Friend: 네게 좋은 북마크 매니저가 필요한 것처럼 들리기는 하지만, 여기서 진짜 문제는 그게 아니야.

Beatrice: 아니라고? 하지만 필요한 정보를 찾을 수 있는 다른 방법이 있어?

Friend: 그에 대한 소프트웨어가 있잖아. 하지만 그러한 정보의 신빙성에 대해서는? 누가 소스이고 무엇이 현안이지? 그런 것들이 진짜 문제라고.

Dialogue 3

Beatrice: 이 글을 봐. 기술과 의학.

Friend: 내게는 무척 흥미롭게 들리는데.

Beatrice: 음, 나는 무서워.

Friend: 왜?

Beatrice: 현재 모든 것이 너무나 빠르게 이루어지고 있잖아.

Friend: 그것 때문에 걱정이니? 도대체 왜?

Beatrice: 모든 것이 제대로 검증받고 테스트되지 않고 있잖아.

Friend: 인간이 실수할 가능성은 언제나 있어, 그건 사실이지. 하지만 일반적으로 의학 발전이 이루어지지 않을 때보다 이루어질 때가 상황이 더 좋아.

Scene 12 (36)

Film dialogue and vocabulary   p. 100~101

V: 아버님께 말해. 우리가…

S: 살인을 망쳤다고요?

V: 살인을 망쳤다고!

S: 상관없어요! 아버지한테 속았어요… 또요! 항상 이런 식이었어요. 말로는 이러면서 실제로는 다른 거죠. 하지만 결국에는… 당신 자신밖에 몰라요!

V: 원래 그런 분이야. 아버지를 변하게 할 수는 없어. 아버지의 의무감을 네가 이해해야 해.

S: 그래요? 아저씨 가족은 그 의무감을 이해해줘요?

V: 아니, 이해 못 했어! 내 아들은 너 같았어. 좋은 학생에, 머리도 좋았어. 나처럼 덩치가 컸지만… 싸움을 싫어했어. 맘씨가 고왔지. 너처럼! 의사가 되고 싶어 했어. 상상돼? 내 아들이 의사라니! 그리고 내 아내는… 그게… 아내는…

S: 둘 다 살해됐죠, 안 그래요?

V: 반년 전에. 그날 밤에 우리 집에 왔던 놈들을 하나씩 찾아서 나쁜 짓을 했어. 오래 걸렸어. 하지만… 너무 많은 의문이 일었어! 그래서 보스가 날 영국으로 보낸 거야. 머리 좀 식히라고.

S: 난 이제 어떡하죠? 집으로 돌아가요? 아버지가 날 살인자로 만들려 했던 건 모르는 척하면서요?

tell Sergey to go back home
V: 그래, 아버지한테 돌아가. 너희 아버지도 늙었고 네가 사업을 물려받아야지. 이 생활에 익숙해질 거야. 여자에… 엄청난 돈에… 사람들이 너만 보면 오줌을 지리고!

S: 고마워요, 블라드. 하지만 그건 납지 않아요.

tell Sergey to run away
V: 아니, 아버지한테서 최대한 멀리 도망가! 짐 싸서 떠나! 난 너희 아버지를 존경하지만… 그는 악마야. 너를 조종해서 악마로 만들 거야. 자신처럼!

S: 그럴 순 없어요!

V: 있어! 나한테도 그랬어! 아주 오래전에. 지금의 날 봐. 미치광이 악당이지. 죽을 때까지 감옥에서 썩어야 할 놈이야.

Communication situations   p. 104~105

Assistant: 안녕하세요, 고객 서비스 부서에 오신 것을 환영합니다. 어떻게 도와 드릴까요?

Dialogue 1
Client: 안녕하세요, 지난주에 커피 머신을 샀는데 작동이 되지 않아요.

Assistant: 그러시군요. 제가 한 번 보겠습니다. 그 동안, 영수증이나 기타 구매 증빙 서류를 준비해 주십시오.

Client: 아무것도 가지고 있지 않지만, 당신네 데이터베이스에 구매 기록이 있을 거예요.

Assistant: 데이디베이스가 얼마나 큰지 알고 계신가요? 게다가, 구매 증거를 제시할 때만 컴플레인이 받아늘여집니다.

Client: 매니저와 이야기할 수 있을까요?